MAKING
METAL BEADS

MAKING METAL BEADS

TECHNIQUES • PROJECTS • INSPIRATION

Pauline Warg

LARK BOOKS

A Division of
Sterling Publishing Co., Inc.
New York

Editor: **Marthe Le Van**
Art Director: **Kristi Pfeffer**
Cover Designer: **Barbara Zaretsky**
Associate Editor: **Nathalie Mornu**
Associate Art Director: **Shannon Yokeley**
Art Production Assistant: **Jeff Hamilton,
Jackie Kerr**
Editorial Assistance: **Dawn Dillingham,
Delores Gosnell**
Editorial Intern: **Megan Taylor Cox**
Project Photography: **Stewart O'Shields**
Hands-On Photography: **Steve Mann,
Robert Diamante**
Illustrator: **Orrin Lundgren**
Proofreader: **Sherry Hames**

Library of Congress Cataloging-in-Publication Data

Warg, Pauline, 1951-
  Making metal beads : techniques - projects - inspiration / Pauline Warg.--
1st ed.
      p. cm.
  Includes bibliographical references and index.
  ISBN 1-57990-712-1
  1. Beadwork. 2. Beads. 3. Silverwork. I. Title.
TT860.W33 2006
745.58'2--dc22

                                              2006001618

10 9 8 7 6 5 4 3 2 1

First Edition

Published by Lark Books, A Division of
Sterling Publishing Co., Inc.
387 Park Avenue South, New York, N.Y. 10016

Text © 2006, Pauline Warg
Photography © 2006, Lark Books unless otherwise specified
Illustrations © 2006, Lark Books

Distributed in Canada by Sterling Publishing,
c/o Canadian Manda Group, 165 Dufferin Street
Toronto, Ontario, Canada M6K 3H6

Distributed in the United Kingdom by GMC Distribution Services,
Castle Place, 166 High Street, Lewes, East Sussex, England BN7 1XU

Distributed in Australia by Capricorn Link (Australia) Pty Ltd.,
P.O. Box 704, Windsor, NSW 2756 Australia

If you have questions or comments about this book, please contact:
Lark Books
67 Broadway
Asheville, NC 28801
(828) 253-0467

Manufactured in China

ISBN 13: 978-1-57990-712-9
ISBN 10: 1-57990-712-1

For information about custom editions, special sales, premium and
corporate purchases, please contact Sterling Special Sales Department
at 800-805-5489 or specialsales@sterlingpub.com.

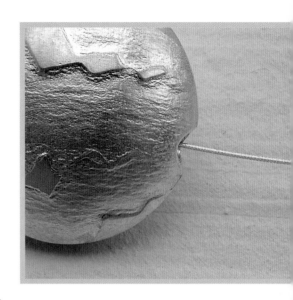

CONTENTS

I love beads. I love to make beads, wear beads, and hold beads. My attraction began when I was a child. I loved the feel and sound of beads as I ran them through my hands. As a metalsmith, I have tried to design and execute beads of visual, tactile, and technical interest.

In the spring of 1975, I was slotted to graduate from an intense three-year apprenticeship to master goldsmith Philip Morton. It was an experimental program based on the European system, but after running it for eight years, Philip had decided to go on to other adventures. At the time the program was scheduled to close, it was filled to capacity with eight apprentices.

After working together so closely, all of the apprentices wanted to make and exchange a symbolic token with each other. We all loved beads. We were fascinated with the small hollow forms that could be interpreted and decorated in a variety of ways. We decided that we would each create seven beads to be traded on our last day together. Each apprentice undertook a secret mission to make seven different beads that would represent him or her in a memorable way to each recipient. For the next couple of weeks, we worked feverishly to complete the beads. We turned our backs to hide them in progress. This project provided a fun diversion from our fears of being kicked out of the proverbial nest.

INTRODUCTION

On the day of the bead exchange, our efforts were revealed. The diversity of the designs and the depth of creativity was exciting and fascinating. Each apprentice now had a small collection, representing each unique personality in the group. The bead exchange stretched our imaginations in form, construction, detail, and skill, and the results would always be treasured.

Katie, a fellow apprentice, and I had become very close friends. We agreed that we would continue to exchange a bead with each other every following June. And we did, for the next 20 years. We used our annual bead exchange as a format for radical experimentation. Our beads were seamless, kinetic, gem encrusted, sculpted, cold connected, made from nontraditional materials—you name it, we tried it. The term and concept of a bead was stretched to new limits.

Collaborative Bead Exchange WHCC, 1975
Necklace, 5 inches (12.7 cm) in diameter
Copper, brass, sterling silver; chased, etched,
hammered, pierced, fabricated Photo by Stewart O'Shields

This book is the culmination of my life-long love affair with beads. In it, I have tried to present a comprehensive instructional and inspirational guide to making interesting and unique wearable forms. Starting with the basics of metalsmithing, you will learn the skills necessary to follow the instructions in the step-by-step projects. You will also become familiar with the tools involved and how to use them correctly and safely. There are instructions to help you finish and string beads so that you will wind up with wearable jewelry pieces. The 40 bead design projects teach you how to make your own one-of-a-kind handcrafted and handmade metal beads. In addition to photographed examples of each specific bead, many talented artists have contributed beautiful images of their own metal bead creations to further inspire you.

Most creative endeavors are a composite of many diverse influences. In writing this book, I not only wished to share designs and knowledge but also to encourage you to incorporate new ideas into your work and expand your own metal bead vocabulary. I haven't invented the beads featured in this book, but over the years I have tried to challenge myself to create different versions, forms, and decorating options. I hope that this book will inspire and motivate you to do the same.

THE
BASICS

Throughout this book there are references to many metalsmithing and jewelry-making techniques. In order to make the projects achievable for people with varying levels of experience, I will begin with a detailed overview of basic jewelry-making skills, tools, and materials. I hope there will be some valuable information for every reader.

Above: sterling silver sheet metal, brass sheet metal, copper sheet metal

Left: roll printed sheet metal

SAWING

Sawing with a jeweler's saw frame is the time-honored way to cut shapes out of precious and non-precious sheet metal. This process can be incredibly accurate. Very small and intricate designs can be cut from sheet metal with very little waste. When working with precious metal in particular, this feature is very important.

Saw Frames

Saw frames come in different sizes, which are designated by the depth of the throat. The throat is the distance from the saw blade to the back of the frame. A 3- to 5-inch (7.6 to 12.7 cm) frame is multipurpose. Too small, and the frame will limit the size of metal you can saw. Too large, and it can throw off your balance when sawing smaller pieces.

Saw Blades

Jeweler's saw blades come in a range of sizes. They all are very small compared to other types of saw blades. Because they are so small, they tend to break easily. This is normal, especially for beginners. Choosing the proper size blade for the job will help reduce the number of blades that break. Proper sawing form is also very important. Saw blades are sized from fine to coarse in this order: 8/0, 7/0, 6/0, 5/0, 4/0, 3/0, 2/0, 1/0, 0, 1, 2, 3, 4, 5, 6, 7, and 8. The fraction blade sizes, such as 2/0, are spoken "two O" or "2 ought."

Ideally, you should choose a blade that has 2½ teeth per the thickness of the metal you wish to saw. Since it is very difficult to measure the teeth against the edge of a piece of sheet metal, for the projects I have listed the size blade you will need for the gauges of metal. For example, 18-gauge sheet metal is best sawed with a 4/0, 3/0, or 2/0 blade. This range corresponds to experience, the type of metal being cut, and the intricacy of the design. For example, the 4/0 blade works better for someone with sawing experience, or for a softer metal (copper or silver), or for an intricate design.

Shears

There are a couple of other ways to cut sheet metal for jewelry making. Some people use special metal-working shears that are much like heavy-duty scissors. This method is more successful with thin sheet metal (22 gauge or thinner). When I use

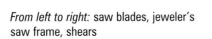

From left to right: saw blades, jeweler's saw frame, shears

heavier gauge metal, I find the shears less accurate. The time that may be saved in cutting will be lost in trimming and perfecting shapes with a file. Frequently, when shears are used, the metal sheet surrounding the cutout shape ends up getting marred. A bench shear (table mounted with large blades) can be used to cut sheet metal. This tool works best for cutting smaller, simple shapes out of a larger piece of sheet metal. Detailed or intricate designs cannot be cut on a bench shear.

SAWING METAL

MATERIALS

Inexpensive sheet or scrap metal of your choice for practice

TOOLS & SUPPLIES

Steel or carbide scribe (optional)
Jeweler's saw frame and saw blades
Cake beeswax or blade lubricant
Saw block, mounted on table or bench

STEP BY STEP

1. Prepare a design for the sheet metal. You can glue a paper design onto a clean metal sheet, use a scribe to trace a shape onto the metal (see photo), or use a scribe to draw a design freehand onto the metal.

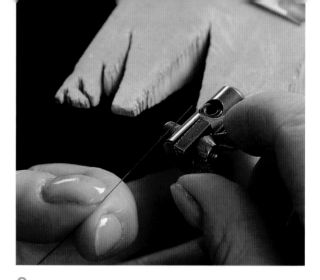

2. To install the saw blade into the frame, slightly open the thumbscrew directly above the handle. Place one end of the saw blade between the frame and the washer. The teeth of the blade should be pointing down toward the handle and facing forward away from the frame. Loosen the thumbscrew at the top of the frame. Push down on the frame as you place the top of the blade between the washer and the frame (see photo), and as you tighten the thumbscrew. It is necessary to create tension on the blade. When the blade is strummed, it should make a high-pitched ping. If it doesn't, adjust the frame at the back to widen the space between the top and bottom of the frame. It will take some time to get comfortable creating the tension and closing the thumbscrew at the same time. Run a couple of the blade's teeth across a piece of beeswax. Don't drown all the teeth in wax. It will spread as you saw.

3. Place the sheet metal on the saw block. There should be a V cut out of the center of the saw block. Place the area to be sawed over the V. This

will provide support for both sides of the metal as you saw. The more stable the metal is, the easier and more accurate the sawing will be. Use your non-dominant hand to "clamp" the metal to the saw block.

4. To start sawing, lean the blade forward against the edge of the metal at a 45-degree angle. Using a very light touch, move the frame downward once, allowing the teeth to "bite" into the metal edge. Once you have cut into the edge, straighten the blade to a 90-degree angle to the metal. It is very important not to press hard in a forward motion. Let the blade glide up and down, using its full length to cut (see photo). Sawing should be a graceful, flowing movement. If you have a white-knuckle "death grip" on the frame, you will break blades and tire quickly.

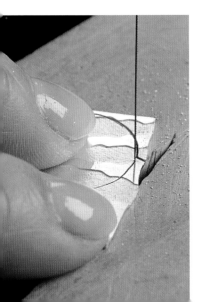

5. When you are almost finished cutting out the shape, make certain to move your fingers out of the way before the blade cuts through the edge of the metal. Jeweler's saw blades make nasty cuts, so pay attention.

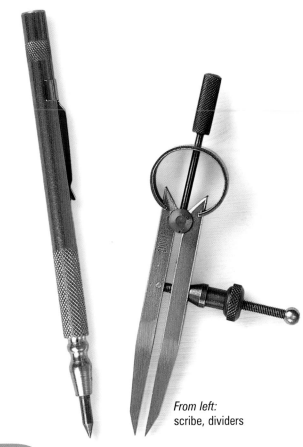

From left: scribe, dividers

Tips

- Placing a light source over and close to the metal will be very helpful. If you angle the light just right, it will catch in the scribe line and help you focus your direction.

- A metal scribe produces a thin, accurate, and indelible line to follow as you saw. Always saw just barely to one side or the other of the scribe line. This leaves the design intact and keeps your sawing consistent.

- Lubricant helps the blade move more smoothly through the metal, thus reducing breakage. It is better to add a little bit of lubricant frequently than too much all at once. Using too much will obliterate your guideline and smear the design on the metal.

- When sawing a corner, keep the blade moving up and down as you turn the frame or the metal. Turning the blade without moving it up and down will cause it to snap.

FILING

Filing is a process used to smooth and shape metal. If you file an edge that has just been sawed, the file should remove the marks left by the saw blade. In many metalsmithing processes, each step you take removes the marks left by the previous step. In most cases this concept means you saw, file, sand, and then buff.

Files come in many different shapes, sizes, and cuts. The shapes vary so that you can select a file that echoes the shape of the form to be filed. For example, if you were filing the inside of a ring, you would choose a file with a curved surface. To file a surface flat, you would choose a flat file. Common file shapes include: flat, half round, ring, triangle (3 square), square, round (rat tail), barrette, slitting, and hinge. Sizes are the actual length and width of the file. Hand files are usually 6 inches (15.2 cm) long with a tang, or narrow pointed end, that fits into a handle. Needle files are much smaller overall. It is always wise to use the largest file you can for a job. This allows you to work faster and more neatly. If you have a broad flat surface and use a small file, you may get gouges across the surface and ultimately make more work for yourself. The cut of

From top: file card, hand files (2)

a file indicates how coarse or fine it is. Cuts are rated from fine to coarse in this order: 6, 5, 4, 3, 2, 1, and 0.

For the projects in this book, a 2 or 4 cut flat or half-round hand file will be appropriate. The same is true for any needle files needed for a project. In Making Beads from Tubing (page 82), there is a very coarse file used for texturing, called a round mill bastard file (rasp).

Files are made out of steel. It is important to keep your files free from moisture or chemicals of any kind. Be very careful to rinse and dry any metal piece you plan to file. Once a file rusts, it will never work as well. There is no easy way to remove rust from a file. It is necessary to clean files from time to time. Soft materials, such as wood and plastic, and metal will get stuck in the cuts in your files. There are metal brushes made to clean files, called file cards. Also, the edge or corner of a piece of copper can be run across the file in the direction of the cut to pick out metal bits.

You don't have to automatically file every surface you work on. If you have sawed out a shape, it is advisable to file the edges smoother before sanding. If you have no marks, scratches, or dents on a metal surface, you may be able to skip filing and go right to sanding. Filing unnecessarily can cause a great deal of work.

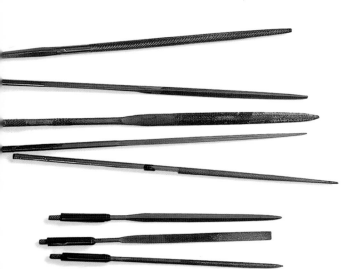

Assorted needle files, texturing rasp file

FILING METAL

MATERIALS

Inexpensive sheet or scrap metal of your choice
for practice

TOOLS & SUPPLIES

Wooden bench pin or file block mounted on a
stable surface
Steel file, appropriate size and cut for job

STEP BY STEP

1. Place the metal to be filed on the file
block/bench pin. The block/pin should be slightly
slanted down at an angle away from the workbench
to make filing more comfortable. Hold the metal
firmly with your non-dominant hand.

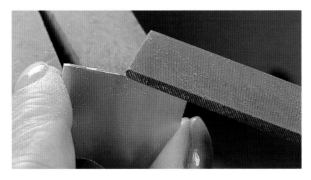

2. Hold the file in your dominant hand. Move the
file forward over the edge or surface you wish to file
(see photo). Files only cut in the forward motion,
from tang to tip for hand files, and from handle to
tip for needle files. If you work the file in the
opposite direction or in a back and forth motion,
you will waste time and effort.

3. If you are filing a large surface, make sure your
strokes cross over each other in different directions.
Filing continuously in one direction may create
deep grooves.

JIMA ABBOTT
Bead in Bead #7, 2005
3.2 x 3.6 x 3.2 cm
Silver, copper, brass; roll printed,
pierced, formed, stamped, tube riveted,
cold connected
PHOTO © ARTIST

PHOTO © ARTIST

Tip

● To refine and control your filing, get close to
your work and try to really see where your
file marks are. The angle of your arm, the way
you hold the metal, and the light source you
use can all impact the accuracy and
efficiency of your filing.

SANDING

Sanding is a process of refining the surface or edges of metal. If you have filed a piece, you can remove the file marks with sandpaper. There are many different types of sandpaper, and the grit can be made of many different materials. The materials I use for sanding have changed over the years. I will describe what I have found to work best for me.

As a student and for many years in my own studio, I used an abrasive paper called emery paper. Emery paper was the traditional sandpaper for jewelers before other abrasive materials became more popular. With emery paper, I would start with a coarse grit and move in progression to finer and finer grits to refine a finish and prepare for buffing. Most of the time I used two or three grits to achieve the finish I desired. However, now I use one grit (400) of a silicon carbide paper (carborundum). The carborundum is very aggressive, yet fine. I am able to go directly to the next step of buffing with tripoli compound and get a smooth, scratch-free surface.

Sandpapers come in many grits and with many backing materials, and most come in 8½ x 11-inch (21.6 x 27.9 cm) sheets. The higher the paper number, the finer its grit. Sandpapers are rated from fine to coarse in this order (partial list): 1800, 1200, 800, 600, 400, 320, 220, 180, 100, and 80. Some sandpaper backings are bonded with waterproof glue. This type is used with water for techniques such as enameling. For most jewelry making, however, it may not be necessary to have waterproof sandpaper. There are also plastic and cloth backings for different applications.

MAKING SANDING STICKS

It is most helpful to have sandpaper wrapped around a piece of wood. This gives the paper a firm support and allows you to push harder.

MATERIALS

Sandpaper sheet, 8½ x 11 inches (21.6 x 27.9 cm), grit of your choice
Wood trim or lath, ¼ x 1¼ x 12 inches (0.6 x 3.2 x 30.5 cm), available at lumberyards or home improvement stores

TOOLS & SUPPLIES

Steel scribe
Stapler

STEP BY STEP

1. Place the piece of sandpaper face-down on a hard flat surface.

2. Place the wood stick lengthwise on the 8½-inch (21.6 cm) edge of the sandpaper and 1 inch (2.5 cm) inside the

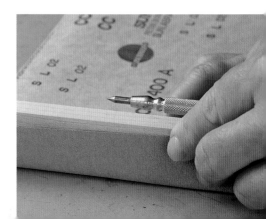

edge. Adjust the stick so that the paper is flush with one end. At the opposite end, 3½ inches (8.9 cm) of the stick is uncovered. This will be the handle.

3. Press down on the stick firmly, and scribe the paper lightly against the edge of the stick all the way down its length (see photo). This scoring allows you to make a crisp corner bend with the paper.

4. Hold the end of the sandpaper tightly against the stick and roll it to the next corner. Scribe the paper at that corner down its length. Continue to roll and scribe against each corner until you have wrapped the entire sheet of sandpaper around the stick.

5. When you reach the last edge of the stick that can be covered by the paper, hold it up and press the opposite edge firmly against the table. As shown in the photo, put three evenly spaced staples into the edge through the sandpaper to hold it securely on the stick.

6. If there is a small amount of excess sandpaper beyond the stapled edge, scribe it until you can tear it off neatly or use scissors to cut it off. Use a marker or pen to write the grit of the paper on the bare wood handle as shown.

7. To get a fresh layer of sandpaper on the stick, tear the paper along the staples without removing them, and then peel the paper back to the next layer.

Tips

- Unlike files, sandpaper works in all directions. To smooth surfaces more quickly and evenly, it's a good idea to crisscross your strokes. The more firm your stroke, the faster you will get the work done.

- It's unhealthy to breathe silicon carbide dust, so always wear a dust mask when sanding.

- Silicon carbide has a hardness of 9.5 on Moh's Scale of Hardness, a standard for measuring hardness for a variety of materials. It can scratch all stones except diamonds, so be careful when working around or near gemstones.

DRILLING

There are many uses for drilled holes. They can be a decorative element, or they can be a functional necessity for techniques such as piercing out a design. Drilling metal is a fairly straightforward technique, and several different tools can be used. The largest and probably most expensive machine is a drill press. There are also smaller motorized drilling tools and the hand drill. The most popular tool for jewelers is the multipurpose flexible shaft machine. It consists of a motor that usually hangs on a hook and is driven by a variable-speed foot pedal. A metal shaft inside a sleeve hangs approximately 36 inches (91.4 cm) from the motor. At the end of this shaft is a hand piece into which many different accessories can fit.

Holes are generally drilled with drill bits called twist drills. They are sized by their diameter, and therefore, the diameter of the hole they drill (see chart, page 153). Drill bits can be made from different types of steel. Materials such as carbide or titanium are harder and stay sharp longer than standard steel jobber's drills. It is important to wear eye protection when drilling holes, as small pieces of metal can spin out and away from the piece you are drilling.

Clockwise from top: flexible shaft machine, drill bits, alternative hand pieces, chuck key, fully assembled hand piece

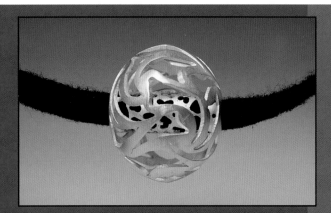

TERESA FARIS
Untitled, 2005
2.54 cm
Sterling silver; fabricated, pierced
PHOTO © ARTIST

BARBARA BAYNE
Two Pierced Pebble Bead Necklaces, 2004
Each, 2 x 1.7 x 1.2 cm
18-karat gold, sterling silver, fine silver; textured, die formed, pierced, hand fabricated, oxidized
PHOTO © PAM PERUGI MARRICCINI

Center Punching

Before drilling any hole in metal, it is necessary to create a small divot to guide the bit at the exact spot where you want the hole. This is called center punching. It is done with a pointed steel rod called a center punch and a utility or chasing hammer. Center punches are usually 3 to 5 inches (7.6 to 10.2 cm) long and ¼ inch (6 mm) in diameter with a tip that tapers to a sharp point. If you do not center punch before drilling, the tip of the bit may wander over the surface of the metal, causing gouges. Center punching is done on top of a hard surface, such as a steel plate. Drilling is done on top of a wood block or some other surface that is strong enough to support the piece, yet soft enough to allow the bit to pass through the metal and into the support without breaking or dulling the bit.

Pilot Holes

When drilling a large hole in metal (2 mm/12 gauge in diameter or larger), it is best to drill a small guide or "pilot" hole first. Center punches make a small

Clockwise from top: wood block, drill bits, cone reamers, burr, drill bits

divot, and the tip of a large drill bit is too big to rest securely in the divot. Starting to drill with the large bit can allow it to "swim" across the metal surface, causing deep gouges. A pilot hole holds the large bit in place much better and makes the drilling smoother than a standard center-punch divot.

CAROL WEBB
Square Donut Bead—Red Patina,
Triangle Donut Bead—Black Patina, 1998
Each, 5.1 x 5.1 x 1 cm
Copper clad fine silver; etched, tube riveted, hand fabricated, die formed, oxidized, bead blasted
PHOTO © RALPH GABRINER

From top: bench pin, steel block, center punches (2)

DRILLING METAL

MATERIALS

Inexpensive sheet or scrap metal of your choice
for practice

TOOLS & SUPPLIES

Safety goggles
Steel bench block
Steel center punch
Utility or chasing hammer
Drill bit
Flexible shaft machine or hand drill
Beeswax
Wood block

STEP BY STEP

1. Put on the safety goggles. Place the sheet metal on a flat steel bench block.

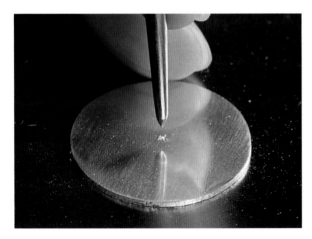

2. Hold the center punch in one hand and the hammer in the other. Place the tapered tip of the center punch on the spot where you want to drill a hole. Hit the other end of the center punch with the hammer once to make a divot on the metal surface (see photo).

3. Put a drill bit of the desired size in the chuck (jaws) of the flexible shaft or hand drill as shown, and tighten the chuck. Make sure the bit is very secure. Lubricate the tip of the drill bit with a small amount of beeswax.

4. Place the sheet metal on a wood block. Hold the piece down firmly with one hand and hold the drill hand piece in the other. Make sure the drill is at a 90-degree angle (vertical) to the metal. Rest the tip of the bit in the center of the punched divot.

5. Begin to run the motor of the drill slowly and steadily, using a firm grip. If you see the bit bowing, you are pressing too hard and may break it. You should see fine shards of metal building up

around the hole as you drill (see photo). Once the bit passes through the metal surface, stop the motor.

6. If the bit does not come out of the hole smoothly, hold the sheet metal down, run the motor slowly, and pull out the bit.

- To successfully center punch a domed piece of metal, make certain to support it under the curve (see photo, above).

- If the metal becomes hot or difficult to hold during drilling, wear gloves or hold down the metal with a piece of leather.

- After drilling, there is often a rough and sharp edge around the hole. An easy way to remove this is to select a drill bit twice the size of the hole, hold it in your hand, and gently spin it over the "bur" or "flashing" as shown in the photo. This allows you to gradually shave off the metal.

NANCY LEE WORDEN
Vicious Circus Necklace, 2002
51 x 5 x 3.4 cm
Sterling silver, brass, plastic; cast, hand fabricated, riveted
PHOTO © REX RYSTEDT
COLLECTION OF JACKIE FOWLER

PIERCING

Piercing is a sawing technique. When you pierce you are sawing a shape out of the inside of another shape without breaking through the perimeter. This process can only be done with a saw frame and blade.

MATERIALS

Inexpensive sheet or scrap metal of your choice for practice (free of scratches)

TOOLS & SUPPLIES

Steel or carbide scribe
Safety goggles
Steel bench block
Steel center punch
Utility or chasing hammer
Beeswax
Wood block
Drill bit
Flexible shaft machine or hand drill
Jeweler's saw frame and saw blades
Saw block, mounted on table or bench

STEP BY STEP

1. Use the scribe to draw the shape to be pierced out onto the metal sheet.

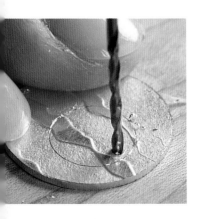

2. Center punch and drill a small hole near the inside edge of the shape to be pierced. (Refer to page 20 for complete drilling instructions.) The diameter of the drill bit needs to be large enough for the saw blade to fit through.

3. Open the top screw on the saw frame and release the top of the blade. As shown in the photo, feed the saw blade through the drilled hole, keeping the design side facing up. Tighten the blade back into the frame.

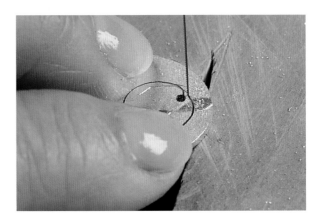

4. Place the metal on the saw block, and saw the interior shape out of the larger metal piece. When you are almost finished sawing out the pierced shape, bring the blade and metal close to the edge of the saw block (see photo). This keeps the blade from slipping and cutting an unwanted line past the design as the pierced shape falls out.

5. Open the top thumbscrew, release the top of the blade, and slide it out of the metal. To pierce another area, repeat steps 2–4.

FORMING

Most people think of metal as hard and rigid, but you can see and feel the malleability of metal by forming it with hammers, pliers, and dapping blocks and punches.

Forming with Hammers

Nonferrous metals are easy to form, and there are many shapes and sizes of hammers that can be used. These hammers should be made of steel and have a polished face. If the face is not polished, any texture on it will transfer to the metal. (Sometimes a hammer face with an irregular surface can be used to add texture to metal.) To spread and "move" metal, you need to place it on a steel surface and strike it with a hammer. This action pinches the nonferrous metal between two steel surfaces and spreads the nonferrous metal.

Hammers with long, narrow faces (cross peen) and those with small, round faces can be used to put decorative textures on nonferrous metals. Narrow-faced hammers create lines or hatch marks (photo A). Round-faced hammers leave a dimpled effect (photo B). All hammer texturing should be done on top of steel to get a clear imprint.

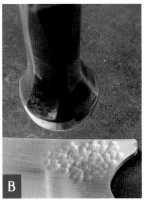

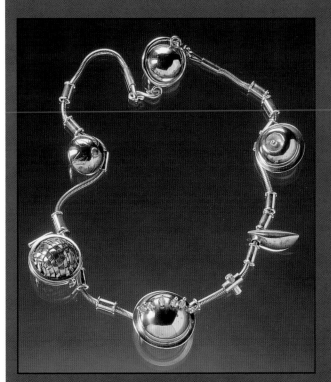

PATRICIA V. BAKER
Space Scape, 2004
20 x 16 x 2.5 cm
Copper, silver, green fresh water pearl, peridot
PHOTO © NORMAN WATKINS PHOTOGRAPHY

CAROL WEBB
Fold Formed Square Bead, 1998
2.1 x 2.5 x 1 cm
Copper clad fine silver, brown patina; fold formed, die formed, hand fabricated, bead blasted
PHOTO © RALPH GABRINER

Hammer Types

A planishing hammer has two polished round or square faces. One face is flat and the other is slightly domed. Planishing hammers are used for smoothing and spreading metal.

A forging hammer, also called a cross peen, comes in many shapes. It can have two long and narrow polished faces, one face that is narrow and one that is slightly domed, or one rounded face and one that is narrow and long. Forging hammers are used to spread metal quickly and can be used for texturing.

A chasing hammer has one large flat face and one small rounded face. The hammer can be used for chasing (see page 49 for a description of this technique), and the round end can be used for forming, texturing, or riveting. A chasing hammer has a specially designed, thin, pistol-grip handle. This gives the hammer more bounce, making chasing easier.

A rawhide mallet has a head that is made of wrapped rawhide. Some mallets are weighted, and some are not. The weighted ones have lead at the core of the rawhide to add weight to the hammer blows. Mallets are used to form metal without marring its surface. Use them to flatten metal sheet or to push metal into recesses in wood blocks or steel forms or around mandrels. Rawhide and brass mallets are used to strike steel or wood forming punches, because their softer heads help prevent the distortion of tool ends.

A riveting hammer has a small steel head, usually with one round flat face and one very narrow face. Use them to spread, and then smooth rivet heads. The narrow face can also be used to create texture.

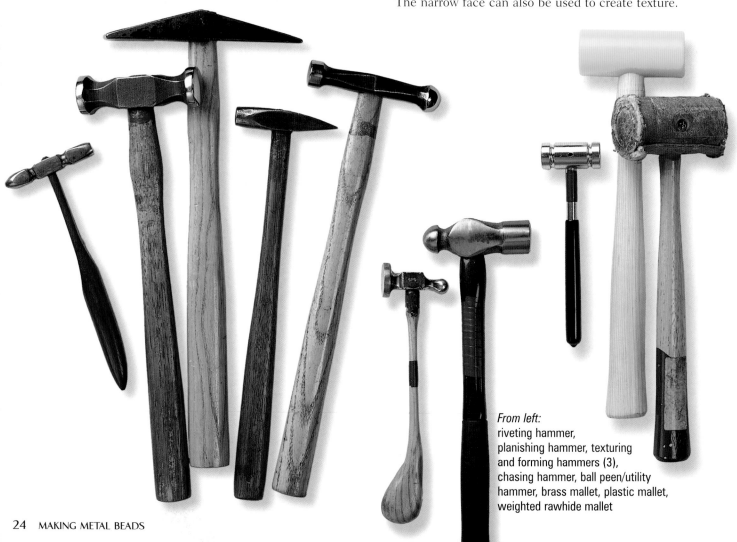

From left:
riveting hammer,
planishing hammer, texturing
and forming hammers (3),
chasing hammer, ball peen/utility
hammer, brass mallet, plastic mallet,
weighted rawhide mallet

Annealing Metal

Hammering a piece of nonferrous metal will harden it. It is possible to hammer a piece of metal to the point where it will crack. If you are hammering metal and it feels resistant to the hammer blows, stop and anneal the metal.

As metal is worked, the crystals within it gather in irregular bunches, bundles, or clumps. This uneven bunching causes the hardness. If you heat a hardened piece of metal to approximately 900°F (482°C), the crystalline formations will even out through the metal, making it malleable again. This process is called annealing. Since there is no thermometer on the metal, you can use flux as a temperature indicator.

Paste flux turns glassy at 1100°F (593°C). Put a small drop of flux on the metal to be annealed (photo A). Heat the metal as shown in photo B, and when the flux turns glassy, turn off the torch. Let the metal air cool for a minute or two, and then quench it in water (photo C). It will not hurt the metal to let it air cool completely. Never put red-hot metal into the pickle. It can splash the pickle, burning you and filling the air with fumes. (For more information about pickle, see page 30.)

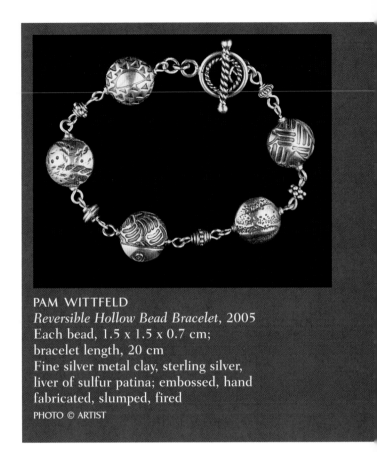

PAM WITTFELD
Reversible Hollow Bead Bracelet, 2005
Each bead, 1.5 x 1.5 x 0.7 cm;
bracelet length, 20 cm
Fine silver metal clay, sterling silver,
liver of sulfur patina; embossed, hand
fabricated, slumped, fired
PHOTO © ARTIST

Forming Metal with Pliers

Jewelry-making pliers come in all shapes and sizes, allowing you to grip and bend metal more easily. It is important to use the right shape of pliers for the job. The jaws of the pliers should resemble the shape you want to form the metal into. When using pliers, it is very easy to make unwanted gouges in the metal. Do not grip pliers so tightly that the edges of the jaws dig into the metal. Rather than using a second pair of pliers, use your fingers to support and help bend the metal. It is advisable to anneal the metal before trying to bend it.

From left:
half-round/flat-nose pliers,
chain-nose pliers (2),
flat-nose pliers, long
round-nose pliers,
oval/flat pliers,
wire snips

Plier Types

Chain-nose pliers have flat inside jaws that taper to a narrow tip. Use them for closing jump rings and for getting a grip in small places. They can also be used to flatten small bumps out of wire.

Round-nose pliers have two cone-shaped jaws. Use them to form small circles or rings (photo A).

Flat-nose pliers have two flat, rectangular jaws. Use them for making right-angle bends and for straightening out shapes.

Half-round flat pliers have one flat, rectangular face and one half-round face. They are used for making subtle rounded shapes and are excellent for shaping finger rings. Putting the rounded side of the jaw inside a curve allows for bending without marring the outside of the curve.

Wire snips have sharpened jaws that clip off pieces of wire. There are flush cutters, side cutters, and end cutters.

Forming with
Dapping Blocks & Punches

A dapping block is a block into which you can form pieces of metal. The blocks can be cubes or rectangles with recesses ranging from hemispheres to shallow depressions. Punches are usually steel or hardwood rods with one spherical or rounded end. The punches come in a variety of diameters that correspond to the recesses in the blocks.

B

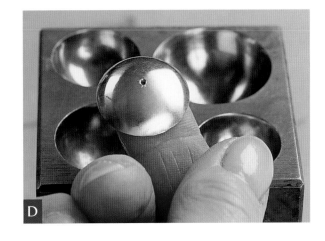

D

C

To dap a disk of metal, place it in the recess of a dapping block (photo B), position the dapping punch over the disk, and tap the punch gently with a hammer or a mallet (photo C). The metal will conform to the recess and become a dome (photo D).

Tips

- When using a metal dapping block and punches, never place a punch over any hole that has a smaller diameter. It is very easy to mar punches and blocks, and it is not easy to repair them.

- Wood dapping blocks last longer if you always use wood punches with them.

- Always wear safety glasses when striking steel tools.

Right: wooden and metal dapping blocks and dapping punches

SOLDERING

The principle behind silver soldering is that pieces of metal, when heated sufficiently, can be joined by a metal that has a lower melting temperature. Silver soldering is important in the jewelry-fabrication process, and it can be very complex and challenging. Practice is the best way to master soldering. This book contains many references to silver soldering, and there are several methods to use. I suggest using either paillon or pick soldering for the projects in this book.

Silver Solders

Silver solders are an alloy of pure silver and zinc. The zinc is what allows the solder to flow. The melting point of silver solders ranges from 1250° to 1490°F (677° to 810°C). Silver solders come in five grades: I.T. (extra hard), hard, medium, easy, and extra easy. When constructing a piece of jewelry, it is best to start with a hard solder, and then use solders with progressively lower melting temperatures for each step. This sequence helps prevent the previous solder joint from being disturbed. If you have more than four soldering procedures on one piece, I suggest using hard solder more than once before moving to a solder with a lower melting temperature. Solders that melt at higher temperatures are more silver in color than easy solders. Overheating silver solder will burn out more of the zinc and cause pitting.

From left: wire, sheet, and paste solders

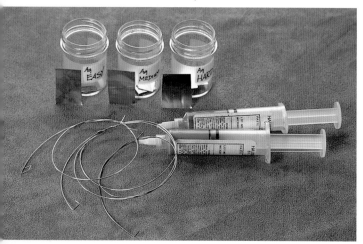

CUTTING SOLDER PAILLONS

Silver solder is sold in sheet, wire, and paste form. All soldering in this book is done with sheet solder that has been cut into small pieces, called paillons.

MATERIALS

Silver sheet solder

TOOLS & SUPPLIES

Solder shears
Small storage container, marked with solder type

STEP BY STEP

1. Use solder shears to cut narrow parallel strips of the silver solder sheet, each approximately ½ inch (1.3 cm) long by ¹⁄₁₆ inch (1.6 mm) wide. Leave the rest of the sheet intact.

2. With the tip of one finger, hold the solder sheet at the end of the fringe. Using solder shears, cut perpendicular to the fringe ¹⁄₁₆ inch (1.6 cm) from the end (see photo). This will produce one row of ¹⁄₁₆ x ¹⁄₁₆-inch (1.6 x 1.6 cm) squares. If more paillons are needed, cut another row.

3. Transfer the paillons and other small pieces of sheet solder into containers marked by solder type for storage.

Flux

Flux is a substance that is applied to the surfaces of metals before soldering. It creates an oxygen-free atmosphere that prevents oxides from developing while metal is being soldered. (Silver solder does not flow well with oxides present.) Flux should be brushed onto clean metal before it is heated to a soldering temperature. It should cover the surface, not drown it. Some fluxes contain fluorides, and some solders contain cadmium, so it is very important to work with flux and solders in a well-ventilated area.

Liquid flux *(left)*, paste flux *(right)*

Soldering Surfaces

There are different surfaces on which to solder. They vary in size, shape, and heat-retaining qualities. For the projects in this book, you will need a soldering surface that is flat and yet soft enough so that recesses can be easily carved into it. A jeweler's charcoal block and a magnesia soldering block work well. Both can be made flat again if they burn or wear away. Charcoal blocks retain heat while soldering, making the process faster, but they can be messy. It is necessary to wrap a wire around the narrow edge of a charcoal block to help keep it from cracking. Magnesia blocks are the shape of a small brick. They are inexpensive and have many of the attributes of a charcoal block.

Metal Preparation

Silver solders do not flow well on metal if dirt or oils are present. There are several ways to clean metal in preparation for soldering. Placing the metal in a hot pickle solution for several minutes prior to soldering, scrubbing the metal with a diluted detergent and ammonia solution with a toothbrush, or using an abrasive paper or cloth are commonly used methods.

Soldering Safety

It is important to have a safe setup for soldering. Always have adequate ventilation in any area where you plan to solder. The table surface you work on must be fireproof. A table with a metal, ceramic tile, stone, cement board, or calcium silicate board top will be safer. The surfaces surrounding your soldering area must also be fireproof. If you have any doubts about the safety of your soldering setup, call your local fire department for a consultation. Filtered safety glasses should be worn while soldering because torch flames can be damaging to your eyes. Safety glasses also protect your eyes from the heat of the torch. Sometimes when a metal piece is heated, the flux will bubble, and a paillon of solder can pop off and hit you in the eye.

Clockwise from top: compressed charcoal block, charcoal block, magnesia block, carborundum grain

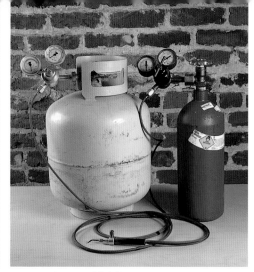

Acetylene-air torch setup *(left)*, acetylene-oxygen torch setup *(center)*, propane-oxygen torch setup *(right)*

Soldering Torches

Jewelers use several types of soldering torches. The most common and easy to set up is a one-tank system that uses acetylene and air, available from most jewelry tool suppliers. Other types of torches use two-tank systems of either acetylene or propane and bottled oxygen. You should check with your insurance company or local fire department for safe and acceptable setup.

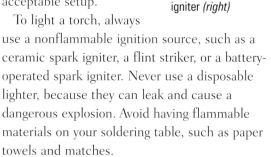

Flint striker *(left)*, ceramic spark igniter *(right)*

To light a torch, always use a nonflammable ignition source, such as a ceramic spark igniter, a flint striker, or a battery-operated spark igniter. Never use a disposable lighter, because they can leak and cause a dangerous explosion. Avoid having flammable materials on your soldering table, such as paper towels and matches.

Pickle

After soldering or annealing, metal should be placed in a solution called pickle, which is a mild acid dissolved in water. Pickle cleans the metal and dissolves flux. There are many commercial pickles available in dry powder form. When mixing the solution, always add the acid to the water. This solution can be used cold or warm, but not boiling. Sodium bisulfate is a common pickle. You can also use citric acid powder, alum, or sodium carbonate (soda ash) dissolved in water. Use copper or plastic tongs to put items into or to remove them from the pickle. Never place steel into pickle, as it will cause copperplating.

Basic Rules of Silver Soldering

- Edges to be soldered must fit together smoothly and evenly

- All surfaces to be soldered must be clean of dirt and oil

- Flux must be applied to surfaces to be soldered

- Heat must be applied to the entire piece, not just the solder

- Silver solder flows toward heat. When soldering a small piece of metal to a large one, heat the larger piece more to bring both pieces to the same temperature at the same time, thus flowing the solder to both pieces.

SOLDERING KIT

Not every bead project calls for every tool on this list. I recommend that you read the instructions completely, and then assemble the required tools and supplies.

Heat-resistant soldering surfaces, such as charcoal blocks, firebricks, or ceramic plates
Soldering torch
Striker
Flux
Flux brush or other applicator
Hard, medium, and easy solder
Solder snips
Solder pick
Tweezers
Cross-locking tweezers with insulated handle
Copper tongs
Water for quenching
Pickle
Pickle warming pot, such as a slow cooker
Safety glasses
Fire extinguisher

BROOKE MARKS-SWANSON
Necklace with Two Spheres, 2003
Largest, 2.5 x 1.3 cm
18-karat gold, sterling silver; oxidized, cast
PHOTO © ARTIST

AARON F. MACSAI
Spirals in Suspension, 2005
3 x 2 x 2 cm
14-, 18-, and 20-karat yellow gold, pink, green, and palladium white gold, 24-karat gold, diamond; forged, filed, extruded, soldered, fused, bound, milled, sandblasted
PHOTO © ARTIST

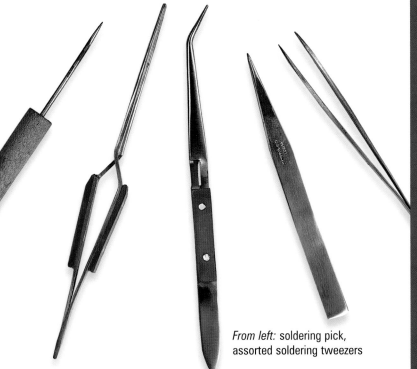

From left: soldering pick, assorted soldering tweezers

Paillon & Pick Soldering

Placing paillons on the seam to be soldered is one of the neatest methods of silver soldering. In pick soldering, paillons are picked up by a steel probe (photo A) and placed on the spot to be soldered as

the metal is being heated. Both of these methods are very orderly and conserve solder. When making beads, it is advantageous to be as neat as possible because it can be very difficult to hold a bead while filing or sanding. Many of the projects in this book are made from metal with a delicate surface texture. If you have to file or sand too much solder off these forms, you may obliterate the texture.

Wire Soldering

In wire soldering, also called stick soldering, a wire made of silver solder is touched to the surface to be soldered as it is being heated with a torch (photo B). This method can be very fast, but it can also be very messy. Because many beads are soldered hollow forms, the wire solder has to be

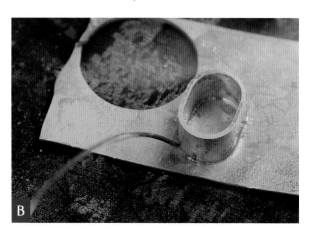

applied from the outside. It can be very difficult to get the wire solder to flow evenly around the outside edge of a hollow form. The interior of a hollow form stays somewhat cooler then the exterior where the torch is directly heating it. Since silver solder flows toward the heat, this makes the application more difficult; the solder tends to stay on the outside where the metal is hotter.

SOLDERING WITH PAILLONS

Paillons are small squares of silver solder sheet. Because you are cutting and placing small pieces of solder onto the metal, it is easy to control the amount of solder that will be able to flow.

Paillon soldering can work for any seam-soldering operation. There are so many different applications for using paillons that it would be difficult to describe all of them in detail. For each step-by-step bead technique, I will describe the specifics of how to place the pallions and heat the metal for paillon soldering.

MATERIALS

Nonferrous sheet metal of your choice
Silver solder sheet, easy, medium, or hard

TOOLS & SUPPLIES

Soldering kit, page 31

STEP BY STEP

1. Clean the metal to be soldered of all dirt and grease. Common ways to clean metals include placing the metal in a hot pickle solution, abrading the metal with abrasive paper or cloth, or washing the metal with a mild solution of ammonia and detergent.

2. Place the metal to be soldered on a soldering block. Apply flux to the edges or surfaces that will be soldered (see photo). Cover the surfaces, but don't drown them with flux.

3. Hold a 1 x 1-inch (2.5 x 2.5 cm) piece of sheet solder in one hand. Use soldering shears to cut parallel slices of the sheet solder, each ½ inch (1.3 cm) long x ¹⁄₁₆ inch (1.6 mm) wide. This will look like a fringe. Use the shears to cut across the fringe, ¹⁄₁₆ inch (1.6 cm) from the end, creating small squares (paillons) that are ¹⁄₁₆ x ¹⁄₁₆ inch (1.6 x 1.6 mm). Important: As you cut the fringe, hold your fingertip across the end so the solder pieces don't fly off and get lost.

4. Use soldering tweezers to pick up one piece of solder at a time and place it on the fluxed metal seam. Spacing the paillons ⅛ to ¼ inch (3 to 6 mm) apart, place as many as you can on the seam. (Usually you only need to place the paillons on one half of any seam, and then put the two metal pieces together. In some instances, such as soldering a rim onto a flat plate, you would place the paillons on the plate where the edge of the rim meets it.)

5. Light the torch flame and adjust it to the appropriate size for the piece to be soldered.

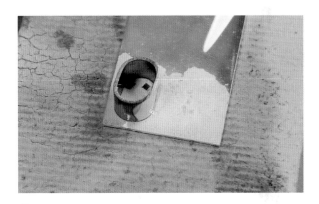

6. Begin to heat the piece very gradually. The flux needs to be dried by the heat of the torch slowly. If wet flux is heated too quickly, the bubbling of the flux may pop the solder pieces off, which can be frustrating and hazardous.

7. After the flux is dry, heat the metal evenly until the paillons flow and a complete line of solder connects the pieces along the seam (see photo).

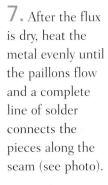

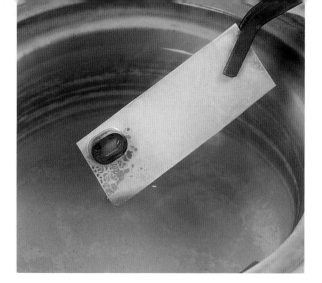

8. Let the soldered metal air cool for 30 seconds, and then pick it up with insulated-grip tweezers and quench it in water. Pickle the piece in hot pickle (use a slow cooker with a steady low heat) for approximately five minutes (see photo). If using cold or room temperature pickle, this process may take 10 to 15 minutes. Rinse and dry the piece.

PRODUCTION SOLDERING FOR DOMED BEADS

When making double-dome beads, it is possible to solder them production style. Many domes can be stacked on top of each other, making soldering a faster operation.

MATERIALS

Nonferrous sheet metal of your choice,
   20 to 18 gauge
Copper or brass wire, gauge smaller than hole
   in dome

TOOLS & SUPPLIES

Dividers or plastic circle template
Scribe
Steel block
Center punch
Chasing hammer
Jeweler's saw and 2/0 saw blades
Beeswax or blade lubricant
Soldering kit, page 31
Steel or wood dapping block and punches
Utility hammer or weighted mallet
Sandpaper, 400 grit
Flexible shaft or hand drill
Drill bits

STEP BY STEP

1. Follow steps 1–8 of The Double-Dome Bead with Centered Holes on page 104. Make as many beads as you wish up to this point.

2. Imbed one end of the copper or brass wire into the soldering block vertically.

KATIE CLEAVER
Untitled, 1997
3.2 x 3.2 x 0.5 cm
Silver, copper, bronze; hand fabricated
PHOTO © ROB SPERBER

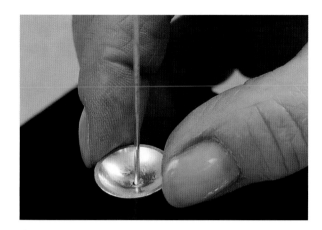

3. Thread one of the domes onto the wire with its concave side facing up.

4. Lightly flux the edges of this dome. Place three or four solder paillons on the edge of the dome as shown, each ¹⁄₁₆-inch (1.6 mm) square.

5. Flux the edge of the dome to be soldered to the first dome. Slide this dome down on the wire with the concave side facing down (see photo). You now have one full bead ready for soldering.

6. Slide the rest of the domes on the wire following the method described in steps 3–5.

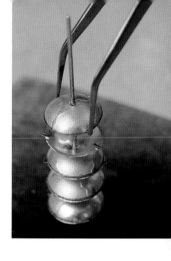

7. Light the torch and begin to heat the stack of domes slowly, drying the flux.

8. Continue to heat the domes, starting at the bottom pair. Heat the base of the bottom dome evenly. As soon as the solder flows on the bottom domes, move the heat up to the next set of domes. Keep moving up the stack until all beads are soldered (see photo).

9. Wait a minute, and then use soldering tweezers to carefully pull the beads off the wire one by one. Quench each bead in water, and then pickle, rinse, and dry them.

Tips

- Heat rises. This process makes the most of the heat from the soldering torch.

- Avoid stacking too many domes on the wire. Always keep the wire straight and vertical.

FINISHING

Metal can have many finishes, ranging from the highly textured to the mirror polish. Deciding which finish is best depends on personal preference, what is practical for the size and shape of the piece, and what detail or design might already exist. A piece with a smooth, plain surface has more finishing options than a piece with delicate detail or a surface decoration.

Buffing & Polishing

Buffing is a process using a motor, cloth wheel, and an abrasive compound to smooth and remove fine scratches from metal surfaces. The best motors for buffing are sealed, keeping their bearings and internal mechanisms clean. A one-quarter to one-half horsepower motor will work well. The motor should turn at 1700 or more revolutions per minute (rpms). Motors like this can have one or two spindles. Tapered spindle adaptors are available to make changing buffing wheels more convenient.

Clockwise from top: polishing wheels, tripoli polishing compound, rouge polishing compound, ring polishing wheel, bobbing compound

Buffing motor

Buffing Safety

Always wear safety goggles when buffing metal. Because this process creates dust and cloth debris, you should also wear a dust mask or respirator. To help reduce the amount of compound released into your work area, I recommend having some sort of vacuum hood that draws the debris away from you and into a container. Although there are many sophisticated vacuum systems available, simpler designs can be implemented using a shop vacuum

and some ducting. Clean vacuum receptacles regularly and frequently change their filters.

Buffing Wheels

Buffing wheels are made with different materials in different styles. I prefer unstitched, untreated, high-thread-count muslin. This type produces a very high polish and moves into small crevices easily. For more aggressive removal of scratches, stitched or treated muslin works well. Most buffing wheels have a firmly stitched or reinforced center hole that self-threads when placed on a tapered spindle. A wheel with a 3- to 5-inch (7.6 to 12.5 cm) diameter is adequate for most jobs. The larger the diameter of the wheel, the faster the rotations per minute (rpms) at its edge. This increase makes it more difficult to hold onto small pieces.

As you face the buffing motor, the wheel will rotate toward you and down. It is important to hold all pieces within the bottom front quarter of the wheel (photo A, facing page). If you hold a piece too high, there will not be enough momentum. If you hold a piece too low, it may be difficult to see and will be grabbed away by the wheel more easily.

Buffing Compounds

Compounds are abrasive grits usually imbedded in a wax or grease base. They are sold as bars or cylinders. Some compounds are available in a

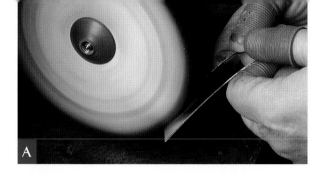

water-soluble base, making for easier removal of the compound after buffing. Compounds are applied to the buffing wheel by touching the compound to the wheel as it rotates (photo B). There should be an even, thorough coating on the wheel, and the compound should be refreshed periodically as you buff. Overloading the wheel with compound will make the compound fly off and won't speed the buffing process. If clumps of compound build on the wheel, they should be removed with a wire brush tool called a rake.

Buffing compounds have different qualities and levels of effectiveness. Since some work particularly well on one metal and not another, it is important to choose the right compound. To achieve a good high polish, it helps to start with a coarser cutting compound, and then move to a finer compound. Always use one buffing wheel per compound. If you mix compounds on one wheel, you will eventually have one mid-range compound. Some softer metals, such as copper, can leave particles on the wheels, and when you buff another metal, streaking may occur. I have one set of wheels for copper, brass, and nickel, and another set for silver and gold.

Polishing Metal

My favorite polishing procedure is to start with tripoli compound, clean the piece, and then use red rouge for the final finish. It is important to clean

the metal before using a different compound. I use 1 cup (0.24 L) warm water mixed with 1 tablespoon of ammonia and 1 teaspoon (4.9 mL) of dish detergent to cut the grease base of compounds. Gently rub the metal with your fingers or let it soak, and then rinse with hot water. Dry pieces with a soft cloth towel. (Scrubbing with toothbrushes will scratch a high polish. Paper towels can also mar a highly polished surface.)

Textured Finishes Using Power Tools

There are several wheels you can use to create textured metal surfaces. Most of them come in three grades: fine, medium, and coarse. These wheels are used without any compound applied to them. Cloth buffing wheels, satin finish buffs, and radial bristle disks are also available in a miniature size to be used with a flexible shaft machine.

Clockwise from left: metal needle wheel, radial bristle discs, satin finish wheel, mini radial bristle discs

Satin Finish Wheels

Satin finish wheels create a soft, brushed finish on metal surfaces and will remove light scratches. They are made from the material commonly used to scrub dishes. The base material is nylon with an abrasive bonded to it. The diameter of this wheel is usually 3 or 4 inches (7.6 or 10.2 cm), and there may be two to four layers of material per wheel. The texture they leave will follow the direction of the wheel.

Metal Needle Wheels

Metal needle wheels produce a very sparkly finish. They consist of a self-threading plastic hub (wheel center) with fine, medium, or coarse steel wires

LINDA KAYE-MOSES
KI (Kindness), 2003
2.5 x 6.5 x 1 cm
Fine silver, fine gold, metal clay, patina;
hand fabricated, polished, finished
PHOTO © EVAN J. SOLDINGER
PRIVATE COLLECTION

CAROL WEBB
Rectangular Donut Bead #109 (Front)
and *#108* (Back), 1998
Each, 7.6 x 5.1 x 1 cm
Copper clad fine silver; etched, die
formed, hand fabricated, tube riveted,
oxidized, bead blasted
PHOTO © RALPH GABRINER

KERSTIN NICHOLS
Polly's Tiara, 2004
7 x 17.8 x 16.5 cm
Sterling silver, fine
silver, 24-karat gold,
22-karat yellow gold,
enamel, citrines,
amethysts, patina;
hand fabricated, roll
printed, punched, kum
boo, riveted, soldered,
die formed, dapped,
pierced, drilled,
textured, oxidized
PHOTO © ROBERT DIAMANTE
COLLECTION OF POLLY AND
DAVE ALLEN

connected to horizontal rods on the hub. It is difficult to get into small recesses with metal needle wheels, and delicate details on a metal surface may be altered or removed with a needle wheel. Wheels with larger needles are more aggressive than those with smaller ones. If too much pressure is applied while using one of these, the needles tend to break off, so eye protection must be worn.

Radial Bristle Disks

Radial bristle disks are made from a very versatile and flexible material and are imbedded with abrasive grit. Narrow, individual wheels are stacked next to each other on a spindle adaptor, creating a

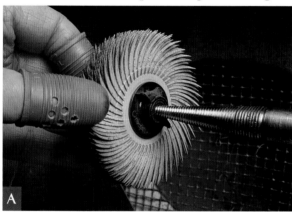

thicker wheel that manages to get in and around details comfortably. The bristle design keeps these wheels cool during use. Radial bristle disks are available in grits from 36 (coarse) to Polish II (super fine). The bristles must be placed on the spindle adaptor so that the ends of the bristles point away from the piece to be polished (see photo A).

Hand Finishes

Ground pumice creates a very soft texture on metal. It is a dry powder that is available in three grits. Pumice should be mixed with water to make a

Ground pumice and abrasive pad *(left)*, burnishers *(right)*

paste. It can then be rubbed onto metal with your fingers or a toothbrush (photo B), and the excess paste can be rinsed off with water.

Abrasive pads are made of the same material as the satin finish buffing wheels. They can be purchased at a hardware store. Use them dry to give metal a satin texture (photo C).

A burnisher is a steel tool with a wood handle. The steel end is elliptical in cross section and should be extremely highly polished. It is usually 1 to 1½ inches (2.5 to 3.7 cm) long and ½ inch (1.3 cm) wide, tapering to a point. Burnishers can be curved or straight at the tip. Firmly rubbing this tool back and forth across a metal surface compresses and shines the metal (photo D). Burnishing will leave fine lines indicating the direction in which the metal was rubbed. It is possible to burnish scratches out of the surface of metal.

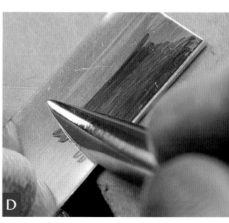

Oxidizing

Some metals turn dark brown to black when they come in contact with certain chemicals. Sterling silver will turn gray black when immersed in a solution of liver of sulfur. This chemical comes in lump form and should be dissolved in hot water. Once a clean metal piece is immersed in the solution (photo A), it usually takes 5 to 10 minutes to achieve the darkest oxidation. Use tweezers when removing items from a liver-of-sulfur solution (photo B). Rinse an oxidized piece thoroughly with water. This chemical has a strong and unpleasant odor, so always use it in well-ventilated areas and keep your hands out of direct contact with it. After oxidizing with liver of sulfur, you can buff or hand finish the piece so its high points will become bright and its recessed areas will remain dark (photo C). It is also possible to leave the whole piece dark. Rubbing the piece with a soft cloth gives the darkened surface a gloss without removing the oxidation (photo D).

Liver of sulfur

FINISHING KIT

Not every finishing technique calls for every tool on this list. I recommend that you read the instructions for a particular process, and then assemble the required tools and supplies.

- Flexible shaft machine
- Polishing lathe (optional, but recommended)
- Stitched muslin or cotton polishing wheels
- Polishing compounds
- Satin finishing wheels, fine, medium, and coarse
- Radial bristle discs
- Metal needle wheels, fine, medium, and coarse
- Ground pumice
- Abrasive pads
- Liver of sulfur
- Tweezers
- Burnisher
- Toothbrush
- Liquid dishwashing soap
- Soft cotton cloths
- Respirator or dust mask
- Safety goggles and gloves

STRINGING

After spending considerable time making one or many metal beads, it is important to string them safely and securely. A string of metal beads alone or one mixed with gem or glass beads can be heavy. I recommend stringing beads on chain, cable, or linked wire segments to make them comfortable and secure.

STRINGING BEADS ON CHAIN

This is my favorite way to string metal beads. The chain is flexible yet strong. A densely linked chain with a small 1- to 1.5-mm diameter works best. Snake chain, wheat chain, twisted rope chain, and foxtail chain are all good choices. Not all types of chain work well, however. A simple link-in-link chain, such as cable or curb, may stretch or break from the weight of beads, and woven cord has a tendency to fray from the metal bead edges.

MATERIALS

Jump ring, 20 gauge, ⅛ to 3/16 inch (3 to 5 mm)
   in outside diameter
Snake, wheat, twisted rope, or foxtail chain,
   1 to 1.5 mm in diameter
Wire, very thin gauge, 3 inches (7.6 cm)
Metal beads of your choice

TOOLS & SUPPLIES

Chain-nose or flat-nose pliers, 2 pairs
Soldering kit, page 31

STEP BY STEP

1. Use pliers to open the end of one jump ring just enough to pinch the very end of the chain onto the ring.

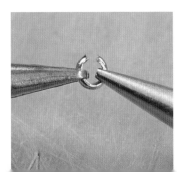

2. Flux the jump ring and the end of the chain. Place one 1 x 1-mm piece of hard silver solder on each end of the jump ring where it touches the chain. Use a small reducing flame to heat the jump ring and chain until the solder flows, connecting the ring to the chain (see photo). Quench, pickle, and rinse the chain end.

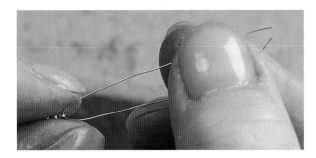

3. Thread 3 inches (7.6 cm) of the very thin-gauge wire through the end of the chain that does not have the jump ring. Bend this wire into a U shape (see photo). This wire provides a rigid end on which to string the beads onto the chain.

4. String the beads onto the chain. If you are making a necklace or bracelet, curve the beads into the approximate circumference you need. The curvature of the necklace or bracelet requires a slightly longer length of chain than if it were to be laid out in a straight line. Use a permanent marker to mark the end of the beads on the chain.

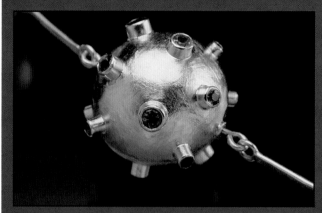

5. Straighten out the strung beads. Depending on the size of the beads, the mark on the chain will probably be ½ inch (1.3 cm) or more beyond the last bead. Thread as thin a wire as you can through the chain as close to the last bead as possible (see photo). This keeps the beads from moving or slipping off the chain while you solder.

6. Use pliers to open the end of one jump ring just enough to pinch the very end of the chain onto the ring.

PAM ROBINSON
Untitled, 2004
1 x 2.4 cm
Fine silver, sterling silver, faceted semiprecious stones; hollow constructed, tube set, hand fabricated
PHOTO © GUY NICOL

7. Grip the chain in a pair of insulated-grip soldering tweezers. Let the beads hang vertically on the chain from the tweezers. Flux the jump ring and chain where they touch. Place one paillon of easy silver solder on each side of the jump ring where it touches the chain. Heat the jump ring and chain with a small oxidizing flame until the solder flows (see photo), and then quench the end in water. Dangle the soldered chain end over the edge of your pickle pot to remove the flux. Rinse and dry the chain end.

TOM FERRERO
Silver Lace Necklaces, 2002
Each, 15 x 14 x 2 cm
Fine silver, sterling silver, gemstones; fabricated, die formed, stamped
PHOTO © DAN NEUBURGER

STRINGING BEADS ON CABLE

Cable is strong and has a simple sleek look. There are many commercial neck cables available in a variety of styles. They are manufactured in sterling silver with different finishes and in plated metals to match gold. Single strand cables come in several diameters. When stringing metal beads, it is best to choose a cable that has an outside diameter close to the inside diameter of the holes in the beads. Always make sure that the beads can slide easily on the cable.

The cables I use have a clasp made from a wire that slips snugly into a piece of tubing. The clasp is not much larger than the diameter of the cable. Since the clasp is so close in size to the cable, the beads can slip off easily. This can be advantageous if you want to buy one cable and change the beads on it. If you want the beads to remain on the cable permanently, however, you have to secure the beads as follows.

MATERIALS

Tubing, inside diameter to just slide over cable clasp
Commercial cable with clasp
Metal beads of your choice

TOOLS & SUPPLIES

Jeweler's saw and saw blades
Medium-grit (400) sandpaper
Chain-nose pliers

STEP BY STEP

1. Use the jeweler's saw to cut two ⅛-inch-long (3 mm) pieces of the tubing. Use a medium-grit sandpaper to smooth and even the ends of the tubing.

2. Slide one piece of the cut tubing onto the cable, and bring it as close to the end of the catch as possible. Use chain-nose pliers to grip the sides of the tube and gently pinch or crimp the tube onto the cable. Crimp the tube so it does not slide, but not so hard as to crush the cable.

3. String the beads onto the cable. Slide the second ⅛-inch (3 mm) piece of tubing over the wire end of the clasp. Use chain-nose pliers to crimp this tube as close to the clasp as possible without crushing the cable (see photo).

STRINGING BEADS USING WIRE CONNECTORS

I have seen many creative and unusual ways to connect beads using wire. My concept of this technique is that individual beads are strung on pieces of wire, and then those wires are connected to each other, much like making a chain. The wires and connections are yet another decorative element of a finished piece.

The length of the bead itself determines the length of wire needed for each connection. For each bead, you will need a piece of 18 gauge (or thicker) round wire that is 1 inch (2.5 cm) longer than the bead. This stringing method only works when there are two holes opposite each other on a bead or when a piece of tubing runs through a bead. (The holes in the bead must be the same size or slightly larger than the outside diameter of the tubing.)

MATERIALS

Round wire, 18 gauge or thicker
Metal beads of your choice

TOOLS & SUPPLIES

Wire clippers
Sandpaper
Round-nose pliers
Chain-nose pliers

STEP BY STEP

1. For each bead you want to connect, use wire clippers to clip off a length of the round wire that is 1 inch (2.5 cm) longer than the distance between the holes in the bead (see photo). Sand the ends of each cut wire flat and smooth.

2. Gently grip one end of one wire in the round-nose pliers where the diameter of the pliers is approximately ⅛ inch (3 mm). Grip the rest of the wire between your index finger and thumb. Gently roll the wire around the jaw of the pliers, creating a loop.

3. Place the tip of one jaw of the pliers inside the loop, where the end of the loop meets the long side of the wire. Place the other jaw tip on the long side of the wire outside the loop. Gently bend the loop back toward the long side of the wire at a 45-degree angle. This centers the loop at the end of the wire.

4. Place the wire through the holes in the bead. Follow steps 2 and 3 to bend a loop on the second end of the wire.

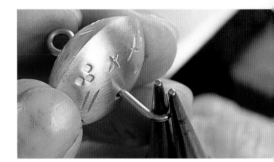

5. Repeat steps 2–4 for each of the beads you wish to connect.

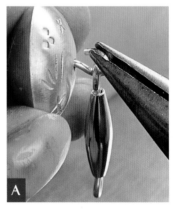

6. To connect the beads, use chain-nose pliers and grip one wire loop sideways (do not place the pliers inside the loop). Bend the end of the wire to the side slightly, opening the loop. Slip one closed loop from another bead onto the open loop (photo A). Bend the end back into place with the chain-nose pliers, closing the loop (photo B). Continue this process until all of the loops are interlocking and closed.

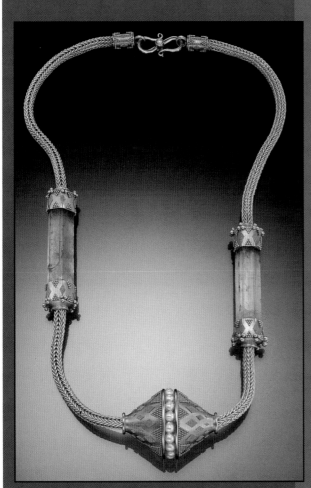

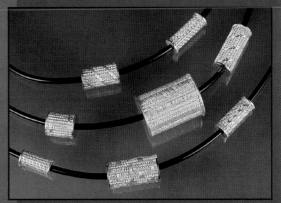

MUNYA AVIGAIL UPIN
Untitled, 2005
Lengths, 0.6 to 3.2 cm;
diameters, 0.4 to 2.5 cm
Sterling silver, fine silver;
twined, fabricated
PHOTO © ARTIST

CLAIRE BERSANI
Gold T Bead, 2001
Center bead, 3.8 x 3 cm
22-karat gold, pearls, aquamarine
crystals; granulated
PHOTO © RALPH GABRINER
COLLECTION OF ALEX TIMCHULA

MAJA
Notice Me Neckpiece, 2005
1.9 x 1.9 x 45.7 cm
Sterling silver, coral beads; hand
fabricated, oxidized, die formed
PHOTO © CAROL HOLADAY

TRANSFORMING
COMMERCIAL
BEADS

Common commercial bead shapes, *from left:* round, roundels, melons and capsules, saucer

Commercial beads are machine made and available in many varieties. They can be seamed or seamless, lightweight or heavy, drilled with two holes or one hole or have no holes at all. They are also manufactured in many shapes and sizes. For the processes covered in this chapter, you'll use seamless, heavyweight beads with one or two holes. The bead shapes you'll be using are round, saucer, oval, and roundel.

Although commercial beads come in different metals, sterling silver beads are the most common. Some commercial beads may be brass or copper with silver plating, but these will not work well with the transforming processes. Most commercial gold beads have very thin walls. They can be extremely tricky to solder to and will not hold up to stamping or chasing. If you find yourself using many commercial beads, it will be well worth purchasing them in quantities of 100 or more, because most suppliers offer substantial price breaks for large orders.

Facing page, top: **Pauline Warg** *Ring*, 1980. 1⅛ x ¾ inch (2.9 x 1.9 cm). Sterling silver. Photo by Stewart O'Shields

Above, right: stamped commercial saucer and roundel beads

STAMPING
& CHASING
ROUND BEADS

Stamping and chasing are simple and quick ways to create many unique designs and effects on seamless round beads. Seamless beads work best because they will not crack or break when stamped. You can construct an entire piece from these beads, or use them as spacers with other elements.

MATERIALS

Sterling silver round beads, seamless, heavy walled, ⅓ to ⁷⁄₁₀ inch (8 to 18 mm)

TOOLS & SUPPLIES

Permanent marker, fine tip
Steel dapping block
Center punch, small steel-tip design tools/stamps, or chasing tools of your choice*
Chasing hammer

*The faces of the tools need to be fairly small [⅛ inch (3 mm) or smaller] or else the bead will be crushed rather than embossed.

BEFORE YOU BEGIN

Never anneal commercial beads before stamping or chasing them. Softening the metal only makes it more likely to be crushed.

Stamps *(left container)*, matting/texture tools (center container), chasing tools *(right container)*

STEP BY STEP

Chasing a Bead

1. Use a fine-point marker to mark the bead where you want to chase or stamp the designs.

2. Place the bead in the recess of the steel dapping block that is closest in diameter to the bead. If you cannot find a perfect fit, choose the recess that is slightly larger. This deters you from scratching the edge of bead on the rim of the block.

3. Hold the chasing tool in one hand. Place the edge of a finger on the hand holding the tool against the bead and block to help keep the bead from rolling. This also secures your hand from floating and missing the mark.

4. Position the bead so that one of the marks is facing up on the topmost part of the bead. Place the face of the tool on this mark.

5. Rotate the bead and strike the rest of the marks. It is important to use the same power for every strike; otherwise, the bead will become distorted and out of round.

Variation: Making a Chased Line Design
To make a chased line design, hold the tool in place and gently roll the bead with the securing finger while making gentle, repeating taps with the hammer. Chasing a line takes practice. I recommend developing your skills on copper beads.

Stamping a Bead

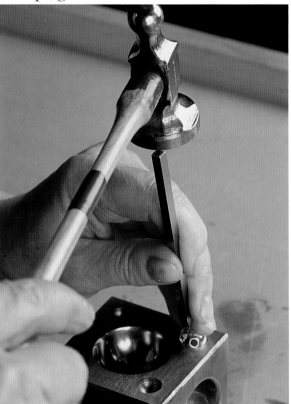

Use a chasing hammer to strike the end of a stamping tool with a tap that is firm but not excessive. The impression of the tool face on the bead will have a slight dimpling around it.

Tip

● Before buffing beads, place them on a piece of wire and bend the wire ends up to secure the bead. This method gives you a good safe grip and protects your fingers. Never hold a string of beads horizontally across a buffing wheel.

ISABELLE POSILLICO
*Time Ribbon Beads
  on Neck Coil*, 2005
Each, 2.5 x 2.5 x 2.5 cm
18-karat gold; hand fabricated
PHOTO © HAP SAKWA
PRIVATE COLLECTION

JAYNE REDMAN
Chrysanthemum Neckwire, 2001
2.2 x 1.5 x 40 cm
18-karat yellow gold, fine silver;
hand fabricated, kum boo, oxidized
PHOTO © ROBERT DIAMANTE

MISATO IIJIMA
Untitled, 2005
Each, 2.5 x 2.5 x 2.5 cm
Sterling silver
PHOTO © ANYA PINCHUK

CUTTING & DIMPLING BEADS

A jeweler's saw is used to cut patterns of fine lines around the edges of a commercial bead (above, left). The dimpling technique is similar to stamping and chasing round beads (above, right). Seamed saucer beads can be used for the sawing process, but cannot be dimpled.

MATERIALS

Sterling silver seamless beads, round, roundel, or saucer, ¼ inch (6 mm) or larger

TOOLS & SUPPLIES

Permanent marker, fine tip
Steel dapping block
Small chisel-ended tool, center punch, or stamp
Chasing hammer
Saw block
Jeweler's saw frame and saw blades, 2/0 to 4/0
Finishing kit, page 40

STEP BY STEP

Dimpling a Bead

1. Use the fine-tip marker to mark the bead where you want the dimples.

2. Place the bead in a recess on the steel dapping block. It should fit into the recess snugly. If not, choose a recess slightly larger than the diameter of the bead.

3. Hold the small chisel-ended tool, center punch, or stamp in one hand. Place the edge of a finger on the hand holding the tool against the bead and block to help keep the bead from rolling.

4. Using a chasing hammer, tap the marks onto the edge of the bead as you roll it with the supporting fingertip. Continue dimpling the bead to complete the design.

Cutting a Bead

1. Use the fine-tip marker to mark the bead where you want to create the pattern of saw lines. Place the bead on the saw block with the marks horizontal to the block, and hold the bead securely with one hand (see photo).

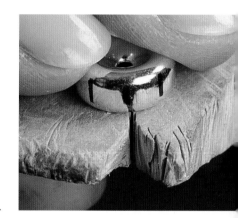

2. Saw the marks on the edge of the bead very gradually. Slant the blade slightly to reach the top and bottom of the marked lines.

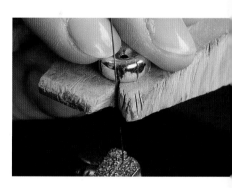

3. Because there will be small burs to remove, give the bead a slight buff or texture-wheel finish.

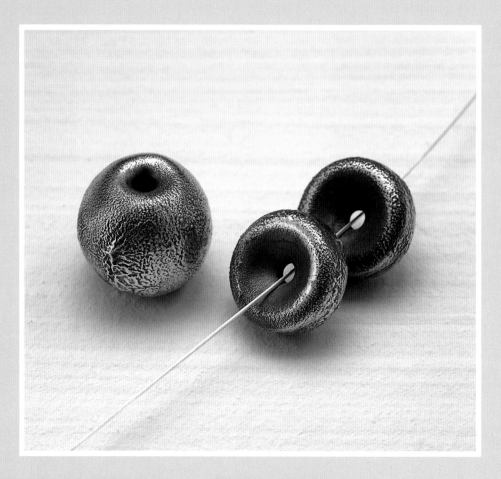

RETICULATING BEADS

Reticulation lets you create a fine texture all over a bead in seconds. Commercial beads that are too small to be altered with any other method can be reticulated. Timing is everything with this technique. Proper flame size and movement are also critical. If you apply too much heat too fast, the bead will melt. Once you master the process, you can reticulate enough beads for a necklace in a very short time. Reticulated beads look great when oxidized and then slightly rouge polished.

MATERIALS

Copper, brass, or steel wire, 18 gauge or thicker
(diameter slightly smaller than bead holes)
Sterling silver round beads with two holes, seamless,
heavy walled, ¼ inch (6 mm) or larger
Oxidizing solution (optional)

TOOLS & SUPPLIES

Wire snips
Round-nose pliers
Soldering kit, page 31
Finishing kit, page 40

STEP BY STEP

1. Cut approximately 3 inches (7.6 cm) of the copper, brass, or steel wire. Use the round-nose pliers to curl a loop on one end of the cut wire. Make certain the loop is large enough to hold the beads on the wire.

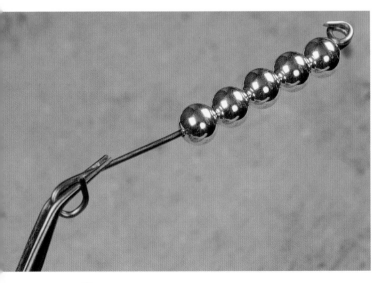

2. Place the beads on the wire. Grasp the straight end of wire in insulated-grip soldering tweezers as shown.

3. Light the torch and adjust the flame until it is small and soft. Hold the tweezers in one hand. (If you secure the tweezers in a third hand, you will lack the movement necessary to prevent the bead from melting.)

4. While holding the tip of the blue flame cone approximately ½ inch (1.3 cm) from the beads, slightly move both hands up and down. You will see one bead become dark red very quickly. To reticulate the bead, heat it to a bright red that is nearly orange. Always keep the bead and the torch moving. As soon as you see what looks like molten bumps, quickly move the bead to work on an area not yet reticulated.

5. Heat and reheat the bead until its surface is reticulated to your liking. The longer the bead is heated, the more fine silver accumulates on the surface, which enables reticulation. Quench the bead in water. Pickle, rinse, and dry it. The reticulated bead will retain a certain grayish color, even after pickling.

6. If desired, oxidize the beads and then lightly polish them with rouge.

SOLDERING WIRES TO BEADS

This is a great way to create mixed metal beads that are not available commercially. Gold wire on a silver bead adds an elegant contrast, and oxidizing the silver makes the gold stand out even more. When soldering gold to silver, always use silver solder to prevent the silver from melting.

MATERIALS

Sterling silver, gold, or copper wire, 22 to 18 gauge

Silver sheet solder, hard or medium

Liquid flux

Sterling silver seamless beads, round, roundel, or oval, 6 mm or larger

TOOLS & SUPPLIES

Soldering kit, page 31

Steel wool or green scrub pad

Round-nose, chain-nose, or half-round pliers

Wire clippers

File

Dapping or dent-removing block and punches, steel or wood

BEFORE YOU BEGIN

There are many design approaches to soldering wires on commercial beads. If you want to solder several separate wires onto one bead, don't try to solder them all at once. It is worth spending the time to solder each wire separately.

Wire in different metals and gauges

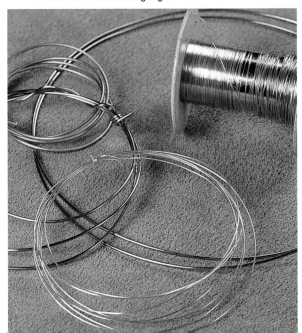

STEP BY STEP

1. Anneal the wire you want to apply to the bead. Pickle and rinse the wire, and then gently abrade it with steel wool or a green scrub pad.

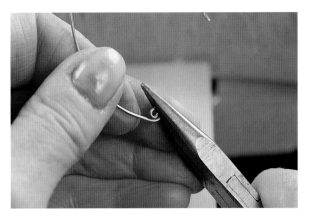

2. Use chain-nose pliers to form a small spiral in the annealed wire (see photo). Clip off the spiral and file the cut end flat. Repeat this step to make two more wire spirals.

3. Place one wire spiral in the recess of a dapping block or dent-removing block. Use a dapping punch to slightly dome the wire in the block. Repeat this step for all wire spirals. (Dapping the wire helps it conform to the surface of the bead and stay in place during soldering.)

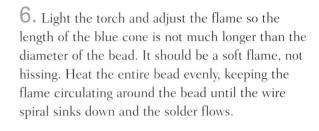

6. Light the torch and adjust the flame so the length of the blue cone is not much longer than the diameter of the bead. It should be a soft flame, not hissing. Heat the entire bead evenly, keeping the flame circulating around the bead until the wire spiral sinks down and the solder flows.

7. If the bead appears to have remained reasonably clean (not too dark and oxidized—you can't see firescale on something that has not been pickled), repeat step 6 to solder on the next spiral. If you doubt the bead is clean, always pickle, rinse, and dry it between wire applications.

8. When all the wire spirals are soldered to the bead, quench and pickle it. Because a hollow form will hold the acid, thoroughly rinse the bead.

4. Cut many tiny paillons of medium silver solder that are smaller than the diameter of the wire. Put the wire spirals on the soldering block with their concave sides facing up. Warm the wires with the torch and apply a thin coat of liquid flux to each wire. Dampen each solder piece with flux and place them on the wire spirals, approximately 1/16 inch (1.6 mm) apart (see photo). The paillons will stay in place on the warmed wire.

5. Coat the entire sterling silver bead with liquid flux. Warm the bead with the torch flame until the flux dries. As shown in the photo, use tweezers to pick up a wire spiral and place it on the bead solder-side down.

Bead Tips

- Soldering: When soldering a bead of any size, first use a scribe, bur, or drill bit to make a divot in the soldering block. This keeps the bead from rolling around the block.

- Quenching: When placed in liquid, a hot hollow form acts like a vacuum. Therefore, always quench beads in water before putting them in pickle so the beads will not fill with acid. If a bead does fill with pickle, place it in a hot or boiling solution of water and baking soda to neutralize the acid.

Pauline Warg *Necklace* (detail), 2004. Necklace, 26 inches (66 cm), each commercial bead, ½ inch (1.3 cm). Persian turquoise, sterling silver, 18-karat yellow gold. Photo by Stewart O'Shields

SOLDERING BALLS
TO BEADS

It takes a little patience to solder balls onto a commercial bead, but the result is classic and very attractive. This technique is also a great way to reuse little scraps of gold.

MATERIALS

Sterling silver seamless beads, round or roundel,
  ¼ inch (6 mm) or larger
Gold or silver scrap or wire (any karat or alloy),
  22 to 18 gauge
Liquid flux

TOOLS & SUPPLIES

Permanent marker, fine tip
Wire clippers
Soldering kit, page 31
Dapping block and dapping punches
Center punch

STEP BY STEP

1. Use a permanent marker to designate places on the seamless bead where you want to solder small metal balls. Place the marked commercial bead in a dapping block recess that fits the bead snugly. Use a center punch to dimple the bead at each marked location.

2. There are two ways to make the small metal balls.

Option 1: Put one end of a piece of 22- to 18-gauge gold or silver wire in a pair of insulated-grip tweezers. Light the torch and make a flame

that is small, intense, and hissing (oxidizing). Apply the flux to the end of the wire. Put on the filtering safety glasses. Hold the wire vertically with the end suspended directly in front of the tip of the blue cone (photo A). The wire end will melt and surface tension will make it ball up. Pull the wire away from the heat and quench it in water. Clip off the wire at the base of the ball.

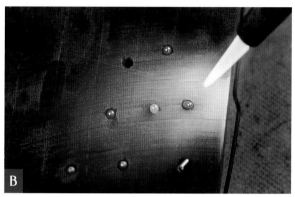

Option 2: Carve a little groove in a soldering block to help hold the metal in place. Arrange small scrap pieces of silver or gold or clipped pieces of wire in the groove. Light the torch and adjust flame until it is small and hissing. Hold the flame directly on one metal piece until it balls up, and then move to the next piece (photo B). Let the balls cool, and then place them in a small plastic lid. Immerse the lid in the pickle. Remove the balls from the pickle and carefully rinse and dry them.

3. Place all of the small metal balls on the soldering block. Warm them with the torch and apply a frugal amount of flux to the balls. Cut one piece of solder for each ball that is slightly smaller than the diameter of the ball. Dampen the solder with flux and place one piece on each ball. Using a small torch

flame, slightly melt or "slump" the solder onto the balls (photo C). Important: Do not re-melt the entire ball.

4. Warm the commercial bead with the torch and apply liquid flux. Place one or more of the small balls, solder-side down, into their dimples as shown. (It's likely that you won't be able to get more than three balls to stay in place at a time.)

5. With a small flame, evenly heat the entire ball until it sinks into the dimple and the solder flows. Be very careful not to overheat. Take the flame off the ball as soon as you see solder flow. Repeat steps 5 and 6 until all balls are soldered to the commercial bead.

Design Idea

To add dimension and produce a more finished look, solder jump rings around the holes of commercial beads.

Pauline Warg and **Fiona Clark** *Choker*, 2005. Necklace, 5 ½ inches (14 cm) in diameter; beads, ½ to ¾ inch (1.3 to 1.9 cm) in diameter. Oxidized sterling silver, 18-karat yellow gold, handmade glass beads. Photo by Stewart O'Shields

ALLISON M. JOHNSON
Bead Necklace, 2002
50.8 x 3.8 cm
Silver, glass; cast, flameworked

PAULINE WARG
Necklace, 1979
Necklace, 50.8 cm; Each bead, 2.9 x 1.9 cm
Sterling silver, amber; chased, stamped

SOLDERING SHEET METAL TO BEADS

This technique is a versatile and unique way to transform commercial beads. You can use sheet metal that you have previously stamped, chased, roll printed, or pierced. Gold sheet or bi-metal works very well. You can also use this process to re-orient the holes on a saucer bead.

MATERIALS

Sheet metal of your choice, 24 gauge or thicker
Liquid flux
Sterling silver seamless beads, saucer or round, ⅖ inch (10 mm) or larger

TOOLS & SUPPLIES

Jeweler's saw and saw blades or disk cutter
Steel dapping block and punches
Soldering kit, page 31

STEP BY STEP

1. Design and prepare the sheet metal to be soldered to the bead. Saw out small metal shapes or cut them out with a disk cutter. For better shaping and soldering, the shapes should be no larger than one-half the diameter of the commercial bead. Clean the metal on both sides.

2. Dap the pieces of sheet metal to echo the curve of the commercial bead.

3. Place the dapped sheet metal pieces on a soldering block with their concave sides facing up. Flux the pieces with liquid flux. Cut three to four paillons of medium silver solder for each sheet metal piece. Place the solder on the sheet metal and heat it with the torch until the flux stops bubbling and grips the paillons (see photo).

4. Use tweezers to pick up one sheet metal piece and flip it over into place on the commercial bead. Evenly heat the bead with a small torch flame as shown until the sheet metal sinks down onto the bead.

5. Repeat step 4 until all of the sheet metal pieces are soldered onto the bead. Quench, pickle, and then rinse and dry the bead.

Tip

- To reorient the holes on a bead, simply solder sheet metal over the existing holes, and then re-drill them anywhere you like. (Use a small bit first, and then enlarge the hole with a cone reamer. If you use a large bit first, it will grab and rip the bead. This applies to drilling new holes on any bead.)

MAKING
COLD-CONNECTED
BEADS

Cold-connected beads are constructed without using solder. Bead components can be joined with wire or tube rivets, or custom connectors can be used to link parts. These beads tend to be quite decorative because the attachments and connections add detail and dimension. Also, the beads are visually interesting when different metals are used for different parts. One advantage of making beads with cold connections is that because there is no soldering, you do not have to be as concerned about aggressive cleanup. Delicate roll-printed or mixed-metal patterns will not be disturbed by cold connections.

Facing page: **Pauline Warg** *Necklace* (detail), 1976. Necklace, 7 inches (17.8 cm)
in diameter; large bead, 1¾ x 1½ inches (4.4 x 3.8 cm) in diameter, smaller beads,
1½ x 1¼ inches (3.8 x 3.2 cm) in diameter. Sterling silver, copper, handmade
Roman chain; pierced, textured, fabricated. Photo by Stewart O'Shields

Above: **Pauline Warg** *Fetish Series #1, 2, 3* (Rattle Toys), 1976. 2 x 1¾ inches (5.1
x 4.4 cm) in diameter, 1½ x 1⅓ inches (3.8 x 3.3 cm) in diameter, 1½ x 1¼ inches
(3.8 x 3.2 cm) in diameter. Copper, brass, sterling silver, acrylic sheet; textured,
drilled, chased, stamped. Photo by Stewart O'Shields

THE TUBE-RIVETED DOUBLE-DOME BEAD

Tube riveting is a popular way to connect metal elements. An attractive, cold-connected bead can be constructed by threading a longer piece of tube through two domed metal disks and flaring the tube ends. The beads pictured below feature pierced and domed metal discs, and the one on the right has a decorative acrylic layer.

MATERIALS

Copper, brass, bronze, or silver sheet metal, 20 gauge
   or thicker, 1 x 2 inches (2.5 x 5.1 cm)
Sterling, copper, or brass tubing, ⅛ inch (3 mm) in
   outside diameter (O.D.), 1 inch (2.5 cm) long

TOOLS & SUPPLIES

Dividers or plastic circle template
Scribe
Steel block
Center punch
Chasing hammer
Jeweler's saw and 2/0 saw blades
Beeswax or blade lubricant
Soldering kit, page 31
Steel or wood dapping block and punches
Utility hammer or weighted mallet
Sandpaper, 400 grit
Flexible shaft machine or hand drill
Drill bits, 0.9 and 3 mm in diameter
2 small ball punches [⅛ inch (3 mm) and ³⁄₁₆ inch
   (5 mm) in diameter] or steel rod with tapered
   cone end
Steel block
Needle files
Small rivet hammer

STEP BY STEP

1. Following steps 1–8 of The Double-Dome Bead with Centered Holes on page 104, make two metal discs, dome them, and then drill center holes.

2. Hold one dome secure and use the ⅛-inch (3 mm) bit to enlarge the drilled hole in the dome to fit the ⅛-inch (3 mm) O.D. tubing. Use beeswax on the drill bit to keep it cool and running smoothly. Repeat this process to enlarge the hole on the second dome.

3. Hold the rims of the two domes tightly against each other. Slide the tubing through the drilled hole in each dome. Center the tube so an equal amount of tubing extends past each hole (see photo). There should be ¹⁄₁₆ inch (1.6 mm) of tubing extending past each hole before you begin to rivet. [If there is more than ¹⁄₁₆ inch (1.6 mm) of tubing extending past the holes, remove the tube and trim it with a saw or file, keeping the ends smooth and even. Feed the tube back through the holes.]

From left: steel rod with tapered end, steel rod with rounded end, six small ball punches

Making Cold-Connected Beads 69

4. Place one end of the tubing that runs through the domes on a steel block. Place the ball end of a ⅛-inch-diameter (3 cm) punch in the end of the tube that is not on the block. Lightly tap the punch with a hammer or weighted mallet until the end of the tube begins to spread and flare (see photo). Flip the bead over and repeat this step to flare the other end of the tubing. This will secure the domes in place while you continue to work.

5. Repeat step 4 using a ball punch that is approximately ³⁄₁₆ inch (5 mm) in diameter. This enlarges the flare on the ends of the tubing and tightens the tube rivet.

6. Continue to hold one end of the tube against a steel block. Use the smooth, flat side of a small rivet hammer to tap the edges of the flared tubing until they become smooth against the top of the dome (see photo). Flip the bead over and repeat

this step with the other end of the tube. The bead is now ready for finishing. The tube rivet not only holds the two domes together, but also serves as a smooth passage for a cord or chain.

Tips

- Use a slow speed when drilling with large drill bits.

- If you have difficulty drilling with a 3-mm bit, try using a 4-mm cone reamer instead. Make certain to stop reaming when the holes are ⅛ inch (3 mm) in diameter.

- If you have used delicately patterned sheet metal to make a tube-riveted double-dome bead, try finishing the bead with a green scrub pad or a #400 radial disk attached to a flexible shaft machine. These finishing supplies will not wear away the surface design and will not require further cleanup.

To connect the notched interlock bead, tabs or "teeth" on the edges of two domes are overlapped. The linked edges are very decorative. Accurate design layout and precise sawing are required to successfully make this bead.

THE
NOTCHED
INTERLOCK BEAD

MATERIALS

Sheet metal of your choice, 20 gauge, 1 x 2 inches (2.5 x 5.1 cm)

TOOLS & SUPPLIES

Dividers
Plastic circle template (optional)
Scribe
Steel block
Steel center punch
Chasing hammer
Jeweler's saw and saw blades
Needle files
Soldering kit, page 31
Circle-dividing template
Sanding stick, 400 grit
Dapping block and punches
Utility hammer or weighted mallet
Bezel pusher
Flexible shaft or drill
Drills bits, 1 mm and larger
Finishing kit, page 40

Bezel pusher

STEP BY STEP

1. Using dividers or a circle template and scribe, draw two 1-inch (2.5 cm) circles on the 20-gauge sheet metal. Mark the center of each circle, and center punch each marked point.

2. Use a jeweler's saw to saw out the two metal disks. File the edges of the disks to make them smooth and even. Anneal the disks, quench them in water, and then pickle, rinse, and dry them.

3. Adjust the legs of the dividers to ⅜ inch (1 cm) apart.

4. Place one divider leg in the center-punch mark of one disk. Use the other leg to scribe a circle onto the disk (see photo). This circle should have a ¾-inch (1.9 cm) diameter, leaving a ⅛-inch-wide (3 mm) rim around the edge of the disk. Repeat this step on the second disk.

5. Center one of the metal disks on the circle-dividing template. Use a scribe or a permanent marker to make a small mark on the edge of the disk at every division line [approximately every ³⁄₃₂ inch (2.4 mm)]. Using a ruler, continue each mark from the edge of the disk to the scribed ¾-inch (1.9 cm) diameter line. (Alternatively, to extend the marks you can position the disk on the circle-dividing template, place a ruler over the disk, and line up the marks from side to side through the center of the disk as shown.) You will now have a disk with equal marks all the way around the edge that are ⅛ inch (3 mm) long x ³⁄₃₂ inch (2.4 mm) wide.

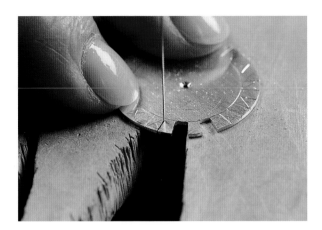

6. Along the edge of one disk, make an X in every other marked rectangular space. (There should be 16 spaces.) Saw out all of the ⅛ x ³⁄₃₂-inch (3 x 2.4 mm) rectangle spaces that were marked with an X (see photo), leaving 16 metal tabs. Repeat steps 5 and 6 to mark and saw out the tabs on the second disk.

7. File the edges of all the tabs on both metal disks until they are straight and smooth. Anneal both disks, quench them in water, and then pickle, rinse, and dry them.

8. Place one of the metal disks in a recess on a dapping block. The disk must fit into the recess completely. Choose a dapping punch with a diameter slightly smaller than the diameter of the recess and place it over the metal disk. Using a utility hammer or weighted mallet, tap the end of the punch firmly and repeatedly, until the disk conforms to the recess. Repeat this step with the second metal disk. Now you have two identical metal domes.

9. If you want to create deeper metal domes, move the disks to recesses that are progressively smaller and use progressively smaller punches. Each dome must always fit into the recess completely. Both domes must be of equal depth and width for the interlocking tab closure to work.

10. Anneal the metal domes and quench them in water. Pickle, rinse, and dry them.

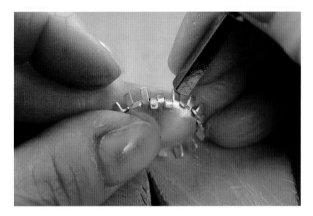

11. Put the two domes together and interlock their tabs. (If you have difficulty fitting the domes together, file the tabs to make them slightly narrower. You may also choose to round the ends of the tabs.) Push the tabs from one dome down over the edge of the other dome with a bezel pusher (see photo). Push all the tabs down until the metal domes are tight and secure.

12. Use a 1-mm bit to drill a hole through the center-punch marks in each metal dome. Using a larger bit, re-drill the hole in the bead until it accommodates the stringing cord or chain. Finish the bead as desired.

Variations
- Make one tab twice as long as the others, and then bend the tab into a bale for hanging.
- This cold-connection bead design works well with patterned sheet metal or mixed metal.

THE
NOTCHED CENTER
CONNECTOR
BEAD

The construction of this bead starts out
like the double-dome soldered bead
(page 104). The seam where the two
domed halves meet has a decorative
edge, much like the notched interlock
bead (page 71). If you want to work
with patterned sheet metal, this bead is
an excellent choice.

MATERIALS

Sheet metal of your choice, 20 or 22 gauge,
  1 x 2 inches (2.5 x 5.1 cm)
Sheet metal of your choice, 20 or 22 gauge,
  1¼ inches (3.2 cm) square

TOOLS & SUPPLIES

Dividers or plastic circle template
Circle-dividing template, page 148
Scribe
Steel block
Center punch
Chasing hammer
Jeweler's saw and 2/0 saw blades
Beeswax or blade lubricant
Soldering kit, page 31
Steel or wood dapping block and punches
Utility hammer or weighted mallet
Sandpaper, 400 grit
Flexible shaft machine or hand drill
Drill bits, 0.9 mm and larger
Bezel pusher
Flat hand file, #2 cut (medium/fine cross-cut file)
Chain-nose pliers

STEP BY STEP

1. Follow steps 1–8 of The Double-Dome Bead with Centered Holes on page 104, using circles that are 1 inch (2.5 cm) in diameter.

2. Find the center of the 1¼-inch (3.2 cm) metal square by drawing a line from each corner to the opposite corner, forming an X. Center punch the point where the lines intersect.

3. Measure the diameter of the two domes made in step 1. Adjust the legs of the dividers to half the diameter of the domes. This is the radius.

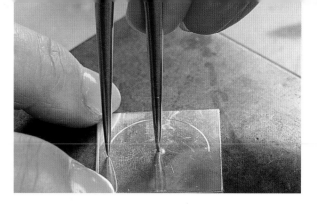

4. Place one leg of the dividers on the center-punch mark made in step 2. With the other leg, scribe a circle as shown. The diameter of this circle should be the same as the diameter of the two domes.

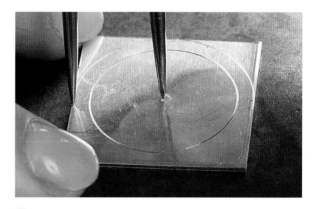

5. Enlarge the distance between the divider legs by ⅛ inch (3 mm) and repeat step 5. There are now two circles scribed on the 1¼-inch (3.2 cm) metal square.

6. Use a jeweler's saw to saw out the largest circle scribed on the metal square. File the edges of the cut metal disk round and smooth.

7. Center the metal disk on the circle-dividing template. Make a small mark on the edge of the disk at each dividing line.

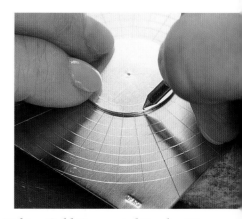

8. Using a scribe or permanent marker, draw short lines from the marks on the edge of the metal disk to the inner scribed circle (see photo). There are now 32 lines, each ⅛ inch (3 mm) long, radiating out towards the edge of the disk.

9. Using a jeweler's saw, saw along each line marked in step 8 to create 32 tabs on the metal disk (see photo). Anneal the disk, quench it in water, and then pickle, rinse, and dry it.

12. Bend the remaining tabs in the opposite direction, each at a 90-degree angle to the disk as shown. (Looking at the disk, half the metal tabs are standing up toward one side, and the other tabs are bent to the opposite side.) File or sand the edges of each tab smooth.

10. Drill the center-punched mark on the metal disk with a 0.9-mm drill bit. Use a larger drill bit to enlarge the hole to the size needed for the finished bead.

11. Grip one of the tabs on the metal disk with the tip of the chain-nose pliers even with the inner scribe line. Gently bend the tab to a 90-degree angle from the disk. Continue to bend every other tab toward the same side of the disk at a 90-degree angle (see photo).

13. Place both metal domes on the disk, one on each side and inside the bent tabs. Use a bezel pusher to push down each tab as shown, alternating sides, until all tabs are down on both domes. Make sure the tabs hold the domes tightly.

THE WOVEN BEAD

There are quite a few ways to use weaving techniques to create metal beads. In this example, two small baskets are woven and then connected to produce a hollow form that is approximately 1 inch (2.5 cm) in diameter. The woven bead can be made smaller, but the smaller the proportions, the more difficult the weaving.

MATERIALS

Sterling silver round wire, 18 gauge,
   16 inches (40.6 cm)
2 closed jump rings, 18 gauge, each ¼ inch
   (6 mm) in diameter
Sterling silver round wire, 24 gauge, 15 feet (4.6 m),
   soft or annealed

TOOLS & SUPPLIES

Ruler
Wire clippers
Flat file, #2 or medium/fine cross cut,
   or half-round needle file
Chain-nose pliers
Soldering kit, page 31
Scribe
Half-round/flat pliers
Hemispherical dapping block
Dapping punch, 1 inch (2.5 cm)

STEP BY STEP

1. Measure and mark the 18-gauge round wire into 16 sections, each 1 inch (2.5 cm) long. Clip off each marked wire length with wire clippers, and then file one end flat on each length.

2. Place one of the jump rings on the center of a charcoal block. Use a steel scribe to make eight grooves in the charcoal block that radiate out from the jump ring and are equal distances apart. As shown in the photo, place a 1-inch (2.5 cm) length of wire into every other groove with the flat end of the wire against the jump ring. (The grooves will help keep the wires in place during soldering.)

3. Apply flux to the ring and the ends of the wires where they meet. Cut four pieces of medium solder, each 1 mm square. Place a piece of solder at the end of each wire where it meets the ring.

4. Light the torch and adjust the flame to a small, soft blue cone. Begin to heat the jump ring and wires slowly. Once the flux is dry, check that the wires have not moved out of place. If they have, push them back into position with soldering tweezers. Continue to heat the pieces using a circular motion around the perimeter of the jump ring. Watch carefully for the solder to flow and connect the ends of the wires to the ring.

5. Repeat the process described in steps 2–4 to solder four more wires onto the jump ring. Once finished, the jump ring will look like a hub with eight evenly placed spokes (see photo).

6. Repeat steps 2–5 with the second jump ring and the remaining eight wire sections. Quench both metal pieces in water, and then pickle, rinse, and dry them.

7. Measure and mark each wire ⅞ inch (2.2 cm) from where it is soldered to the jump ring. These marks will help you keep all the wires the same length when a ball is melted on each end.

8. Light the torch and adjust the flame to a small blue cone. The flame should have a slight hissing sound (oxidizing flame). Hold one of the jump rings in a pair of insulated-grip soldering tweezers. Hold the tip of one of the wires directly in front of the tip of the blue cone until the end melts into a ball at the ⅞-inch (2.2 cm) mark (see photo). Remove the wire from the heat immediately. Repeat this process to ball the ends of all remaining wires on both jump rings. Quench, pickle, rinse, and dry both metal pieces.

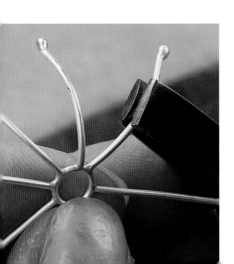

9. Use half-round/flat pliers to gently curve the wires on each piece, creating a bowl shape with the jump ring as the base.

10. Use your fingers to push one of the spoke wire shapes into a recess in a dapping block that has a 1-inch (2.5 cm) diameter (see photo). Tap the wire shape into the recess with the 1-inch (2.5 cm) dap. Repeat this process with the second wire shape. Use your fingers to adjust the distance between the cupped wires on both pieces, making sure they are equal.

11. Use wire clippers to cut the 24-gauge sterling silver wire into two 7½-foot-long (2.3 m) pieces. Gently bend both pieces of wire in half so each side of the bend is 3¾ feet (1.1 m) long.

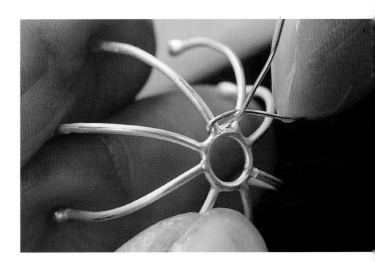

12. Place the fold of one 24-gauge wire at the base of one of the 18-gauge wires, next to the jump ring. Make a tight loop with the thinner, 24-gauge folded wire around the 18-gauge wire as shown. At this point, you are ready to start weaving.

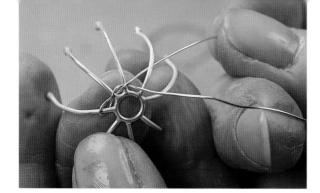

13. Hold the cupped spoke metal piece in one hand, and hold the two sides of the thinner wire in the other. As you turn the spoke piece counterclockwise (if you are right handed), move the 24-gauge wires clockwise with one on the outside of a spoke and one on the inside of the same spoke. As the next spoke comes around, change the position of the 24-gauge wires (see photo). If the long lengths of extra wire become twisted and tangled as you weave, carefully and gently untwist them. If the wires kink, very gently straighten and smooth them.

14. Continue weaving, alternating the thin wire inside and outside of the spokes, until you come to within ⅛ inch (3 mm) of their balled ends. Depending upon the amount of tension you use as your weave, you may or may not use the whole length of 24-gauge wire.

15. At the end of the weaving, use chain-nose pliers to tightly twist the 24-gauge wire around the 18-gauge wire as shown. Leave the twist on the inside of the "basket" so it will be hidden from view when the bead is completed.

16. Repeat steps 12–15 with the second spoke wire piece and the second length of bent 24-gauge wire.

17. Use chain-nose pliers to bend the end of each of the balled 18-gauge wires at a right angle away from the inside of the wire baskets, just above the weaving.

18. Place the two woven wire baskets together with their balled ends touching. Use chain-nose pliers to twist together a pair of 18-gauge wires, one from one basket and one from the other. Twist all eight pairs to join the baskets and complete the bead.

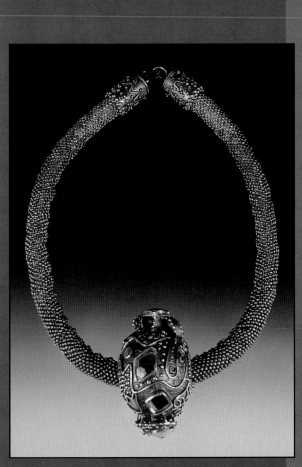

VERNA HOLLAND
Untitled, 2001
21 x 21 x 5 cm
Sterling silver, antique watch crystals,
seed beads; core cast, cast, fabricated,
peyote stitched
PHOTO © DANIEL GRYCH

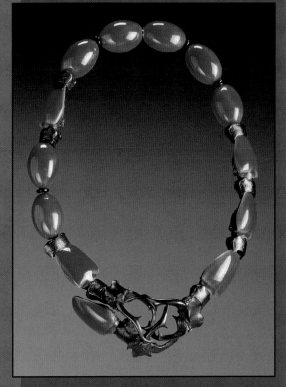

DAVID C. FREDA
Stag Beetles in the Red Neckpiece, 2000
22.9 x 14 x 3.8 cm
Fine silver, sterling silver, 18-karat yellow
gold, enamel; hollow-core cast, fabricated,
hammer textured
PHOTO © STORM PHOTO, KINGSTON, NEW YORK
COLLECTION OF STEPHEN HABERSTROH, NEW YORK

BEADS FROM TUBING

You can use commercial seamless tubing as a base for a variety of bead forms. Seamless tubing is readily available from metal refineries, jewelry supply companies, and some gem suppliers. Tubing is manufactured with different wall thickness and comes in different shapes. Most of the techniques I cover work best with medium- or thick-walled tubing. A thick wall provides you with a stronger material that will not bend or dent easily. A thick wall allows the tube to be textured and etched without compromising its integrity. For the following examples, I used round or square tubing to make the beads, but triangular or hexagonal tubing would also work well. Asymmetrical tubing may not yield good results for some of these designs.

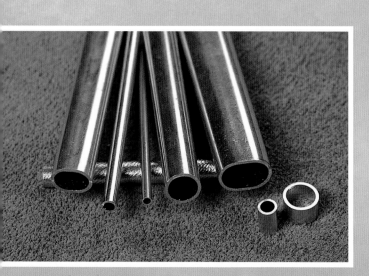

Commercial tubing in assorted shapes and wall thicknesses

Pauline Warg *Reversible Bead Necklace* (detail), 2005. Necklace, 7 inches (17.8 cm) in diameter; Beads, ½ x ½ inch (1.3 x 1.3 cm) and ⅜ x ⅜ inch (9.5 x 9.5 mm). Sterling silver, 22-karat yellow gold; chased, roll printed, hammered, handmade chain. Photo by Stewart O'Shields

THE BASIC
TUBE BEAD

Commercial tubing is available in many metals and in many profiles, making the tube bead a very useful and flexible design. Once you understand the basic construction method, you can alter the body of the bead with surface-design techniques or change the shape of the end caps.

MATERIALS

Seamless square or round tubing in metal of your choice, ⁵⁄₃₂ inch (4 mm) in diameter or larger, medium or thick wall, minimum of ¼ inch (6 mm) tubing per bead

Sheet metal of your choice, 20 gauge, 1 inch (2.5 cm) square per bead

TOOLS & SUPPLIES

Steel ruler
Dividers or tube jig
Jeweler's saw and saw blades
Saw block
Steel block
Steel dapping punch or flaring tool
Chasing hammer
Plastic circle template or dividers
Scribe
Needle files or sandpaper
Disk cutter (optional)
Center punch
Flexible shaft machine or hand drill
Drill bits
Soldering kit, page 31
Dapping block and punches (optional)

Tube jigs *(left and center)*, disk cutter *(right)*

STEP BY STEP

Making the Body of the Bead

1. Determine how long you want to make the bead. A good size range is from ½ to 1 inch (1.3 to 2.5 cm). If you make the bead too long, it may bend during flaring.

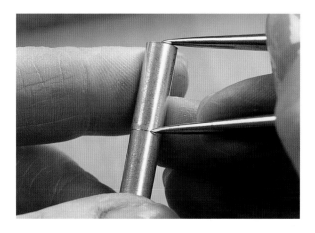

2. Make sure the end of the tubing is straight, flat, and even. Adjust the legs of dividers to the length of the bead. Place one leg of the dividers on the top of the end of the tubing. Spin the tubing and, with the other leg of the dividers, scribe around the tube as shown. (If using a tube jig, adjust the end of the jig to the desired measurement. Place tubing in the jig and saw off a length of the tubing.)

3. Place the scribed tubing horizontally on the saw block. Saw on the scribed line all the way around the tube just enough to score it. Then, saw all the way through the tube. (If you saw straight through the tube without scoring it first, the blade will veer off the mark and cut at an angle. Cutting this way may also break saw blades.)

4. Place the tube on its end on a steel block. Choose a steel dapping punch or other flaring tool with an end slightly larger than the diameter of the tube. Hold the punch securely in the end of the tube as shown. Use a chasing hammer to gently tap the end of the punch until the end of the tube flares. Turn the tube over and repeat.

Creating the End Caps
Flat End Caps

1. To determine the size of the disks, first measure the ends of the flared tubes. The diameter of the disks should be between ¹⁄₁₆ and ¼ inch (1.6 and 6 mm) larger than the end of the flared tube. Use a circle template or a pair of dividers to mark the two disks on the sheet metal, and then mark the center of both disks.

2. Saw out the disks and smooth the cut edges with a file or sandpaper. (If using a disk cutter as shown in the photo, punch out two disks of the correct size and mark the centers.)

3. Dimple the center of each disk with a center punch and drill a small hole at each point. (This hole allows the bead to be strung and allows gas to escape during soldering. The hole can be enlarged later if necessary.)

4. Stand the piece of tubing on end on a clean, flat soldering block. Flux the top end of the tube.

5. Place the two disks on a soldering block, and apply a thin layer of flux. Put three paillons of medium silver solder on each disk. Use soldering tweezers to pick up one of the disks and place it solder-side down on the end of the tube (see photo).

6. Light the torch and adjust the flame to a small, neat blue cone. Heat the tube evenly until the solder melts and the end cap sinks down. Do not overheat the tubing as it may melt quickly. Turn the tubing over, and solder on the second end cap. Wait 30 seconds, and then quench the bead in water. Pickle the bead, then rinse and dry it.

7. If you want the end caps to be flush, file the edges of the disks to meet the edge of the flare on the tube. Use sandpaper to smooth the file marks.

Concave or Convex End Caps

1. Repeat steps 1–3 of Making a Flat End Cap (page 86).

2. Place one disk in a recess on the dapping block. The disk must fit entirely in the recess. Select a dapping punch that fits completely into the same recess.

3. Hold the dapping punch over the disk in the recess. Use a hammer to gently and repeatedly tap the end of the punch until the disk conforms to the recess. Remove the disk, which is now a dome, from the block.

4. Repeat steps 2 and 3 to form the second disk.

5. To make a concave end cap, place the solder on the convex curve of the dome, place the dome onto the end of the tube with the convex side down, and solder (photo A). To make a convex end cap, place the solder in the concave end of the dome, place the dome onto the end of the tube with the concave side down, and solder (photo B).

Pauline Warg *Necklace* (detail), 2000. Necklace, 6½ inches (16.5 cm) in diameter; Turquoise beads, ½ x ½ inch (1.3 x 1.3 cm). Chinese turquoise, sterling silver, 14-karat gold; fabricated. Photo by Stewart O'Shields

EMBELLISHING TUBE BEADS WITH COLD TECHNIQUES

It's very easy to texture beads made from commercial tubing without soldering. Cold techniques, such as filing, grinding, drilling holes, chasing, stamping, or matting are just a few of the ways you can add a decorative touch. If you wish to use multiple techniques on the same piece of tubing, file first, and then drill and/or stamp the metal.

ADDING TEXTURE WITH A RASP FILE

MATERIALS

Seamless tubing of your choice, medium or heavy walled, 3 mm in diameter or larger, cut to desired length and ends filed

TOOLS & SUPPLIES

Small round or rat-tail rasp file (available from hardware stores)

STEP BY STEP

1. Hold the tubing on your bench securely. Make short, sweeping strokes across the surface of the tubing with the rasp file.

2. Continue to file the entire surface evenly in the same direction to create a very sparkly texture.

ADDING TEXTURE WITH A GRINDER OR BUR

MATERIALS

Scrap sheet metal
Seamless tubing of your choice, medium or heavy walled, 3 mm in diameter or larger, cut to desired length and ends filed

TOOLS & SUPPLIES

Assorted grinders or bur attachments
Flexible shaft machine
Finger cots (optional)

STEP BY STEP

1. Insert a grinder or bur attachment in the flexible shaft and try it out on a piece of scrap metal. Experiment with several attachments to find the one you want before you start to texture the tubing.

2. Hold the tubing securely against your bench. Use the grinder or bur to lightly and evenly grind across the tubing (see photo). Turn the tubing to blend the texture completely. Do not run the flexible shaft too fast, because the bur can slip and cut you. Wearing finger cots may prevent a mishap.

DRILLING DECORATIVE HOLES

MATERIALS

Seamless tubing of your choice, medium or heavy walled, ⅛ inch (3 mm) in diameter or larger, cut to desired length and ends filed

TOOLS & SUPPLIES

Permanent marker, fine tip
Mandrel to match inside diameter of tube (a steel rod or the smooth end of a large drill bit works well)
Ring bending/forming block
Center punch
Chasing hammer
Flexible shaft machine
Assorted drill bits

Wooden ring bending/forming block *(left)*, steel ring bending/forming block *(right)*

STEP BY STEP

1. Determine where you want to drill decorative holes on the tubing and mark these spots with a permanent marker. Thread the mandrel inside the tubing. Place the tubing in a depression on a bending block for support.

2. Hold the center punch securely on a spot marked in step 1, and strike the punch with a hammer, creating a dimple (see photo). Dimple all of the marked spots, and then remove the mandrel.

3. Choose the drill bit you want to use to make the holes. It should be no larger than approximately one-third of the diameter of the tubing, or else the bit will tend to slip when drilling. Hold the tube firmly on a wood, leather, or rubber surface with a dimple facing up, and drill the hole (see photo). Repeat this process to drill each dimpled spot. Be careful—the tube may become hot from drilling.

CHASING, STAMPING, OR MATTING

MATERIALS

Seamless tubing of your choice, medium or
heavy walled, ⅛ inch (3 mm) in diameter or larger,
cut to desired length and ends filed

TOOLS & SUPPLIES

Mandrel to match inside diameter of tube (a steel rod
or large drill bit works well)
Ring bending/forming block
Chasing, stamping, or matting tools of your choice
Chasing hammer

STEP BY STEP

1. Thread the mandrel inside the tubing. (The more
snug the fit of the mandrel, the better.) Place the
tubing in a depression on a bending block for support.

2. Choose the chasing, stamping, or matting
tools you wish to use. The faces of the stamping
tools should not be very large. If you choose a tool
with a face that is too large, the impression will
not be complete.

3. Hold the tool with
the thumb, index finger,
and middle finger of one
hand. Use the ring finger
of the same hand to
secure tube in the block.
Strike the tool firmly with
the hammer to get a good
impression (see photo).
If chasing, roll the tube
slightly to make a
continuous line.

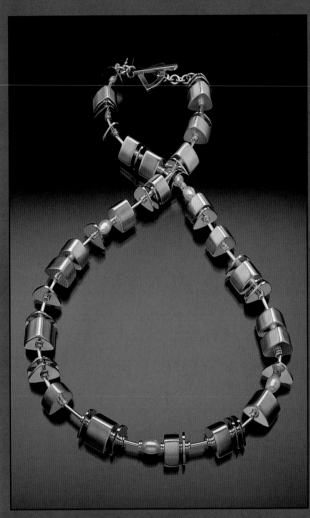

CORINNE FLOYD
Tri-Color Gold Neckpiece, 2003
42.5 x 1 x 1 cm
18-karat gold, 14-karat gold, sterling
silver, white freshwater pearls; shaped,
constructed, formed
PHOTO © JEFF SCOVIL

EMBELLISHING
TUBE BEADS WITH
JUMP RINGS

This technique allows you to suspend

moving parts from the middle of a tube.

It's a simple way to create very unique

tube beads or spacers.

MATERIALS

Seamless tubing of your choice, ⅛ inch (3 mm) or
    larger in outside diameter (O.D.)
Wire of your choice, 22 to 16 gauge (round, square,
    beaded, patterned, or twisted wire can be used)
Liquid flux

TOOLS & SUPPLIES

Jeweler's saw and saw blades
Mandrel, 3.5 mm in diameter or larger
Wire clippers
Round-nose or chain-nose pliers, 2 pairs
Soldering kit, page 31
Scrap copper or brass wire
Flat hand file, #2
Sandpaper, 400 grit, on sanding stick
Steel block
Small punch or flaring tool
Chasing hammer

Decorative commercial wire, *from left:* beaded,
square, twisted (3)

STEP BY STEP

1. Use the jeweler's saw to cut the tubing into the
desired lengths. Using plain or decorative wire,
make a coil around the mandrel for jump rings. The
mandrel should be approximately ¹⁄₁₆ to ³⁄₃₂ inch
(1.6 to 2.3 mm) larger in diameter than the tubing.

2. Use the jeweler's saw to saw apart the wire coil
into individual jump rings. Use two pairs of chain-
nose or flat-nose pliers to close the jump rings,
making their ends flush.

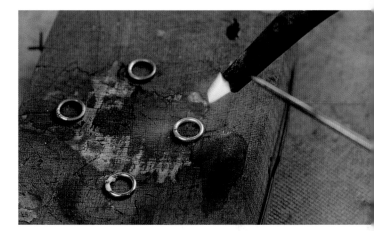

3. Place all of the jump rings on a soldering block
and space them apart slightly. Apply flux to the
seam of each jump ring. Either place a small paillon
of hard solder on each seam or cut the paillons and
place them on a block for pick soldering. Light the
torch and solder each jump ring shut as shown.

4. Pick up the soldered jump rings with tweezers
and place them on a piece of copper or brass wire.
Twist the ends of the wire closed to make a loop.
Pickle, rinse, and dry the rings. (It is easier to
remove the rings from the pickle when they are on
a wire loop than it is to individually fish them out of
the bath.)

5. Flare one end of one cut tubing piece (photo A). String several jump rings on the tube, and then flare the other end of the tubing (photo B). The tube's flared ends secure the rings. Repeat this step to make as many beads as you wish.

Pauline Warg *Bracelet* (detail), 1990. 7 inches (15.2 cm) long; beads, ¼ inch (6 mm) in diameter. Sterling silver, copper, brass; fabricated. Photo by Stewart O'Shields

THE
WIRE-WRAPPED
TUBE BEAD

It's easy to add dimension and interest to commercial tubing with wire decorations. You can add even more detail by choosing patterned, twisted, or beaded wire. Use tubing with any wall thickness for these techniques. If you choose thin-walled tubing, be careful not to overheat during the soldering process. Some thin-wall tubing may melt easily.

MATERIALS

Tubing of your choice, ⅛ inch (3 mm) or larger outside
 diameter (O.D.)
Round wire in metal of your choice, 20 to 16 gauge

TOOLS & SUPPLIES

Jeweler's saw and saw blades
Hand file, #2
Sandpaper, 400 grit, on sanding stick
Soldering kit, page 31
Small mandrel, same diameter as outside diameter
 (O.D.) of tubing; options include steel rod, wood
 dowel, drill bit
Vise
Wire clippers
Round-nose or chain-nose pliers
Round bezel mandrel (optional)

STEP BY STEP

1. Use the jeweler's saw to cut the tubing to the
desired length for the bead. File or sand the cut
ends smooth and even.

2. Anneal the 20- to
16-gauge wire. Place the
base of the mandrel and
the very end of the wire
in the vise as shown,
and tighten the jaws.
This secures the wire as
it is wrapped around
the mandrel.

3. If you want
to create several
spirals, make a
coil around the
mandrel as shown.
This saves you
time and materials.
It takes approxi-
mately three full
revolutions
around the
mandrel to make
one wire spiral.

4. Remove the wire and
mandrel from the vise.
Pull the mandrel out of
the coil. Use wire clippers
to remove crushed wire
that was pinched against
the mandrel in the vise.
Gently pull on the coil to
separate the rings (see
photo). With wire
clippers, cut the wire coil
at the desired length for
one spiral.

5. Use your fingers or chain-nose pliers to separate
the spiral, making it as tight or loose as desired.

6. Use a corkscrew-like
winding motion to fit
the wire spiral snugly
onto the tubing. If the
spiral is too tight to
twist over the tube, put
the spiral on a round
bezel mandrel and

slightly expand its inside diameter. However, it is preferable to twist the wire onto the tubing, because this will give it the tightest fit.

7. Set the wire-wrapped tube on a soldering block. Apply a light coat of flux to the tube and wire. (Excess flux will cause the solder to move too much.)

8. Cut 1-mm-square paillons of hard or medium silver solder. Carefully position the solder pieces on edge against the wire where it touches the tube (see photo). One piece of solder every ⅛ inch (3 mm) should work well. If too much solder is used, the cleanup will be difficult. If not enough solder is used, the wire may bend or catch on fabric.

9. Light the torch and evenly heat the wire-wrapped tube. Watch carefully and remove heat as soon as you see the solder flow. Quench the tube in water. Pickle, rinse, and dry the tube.

10. Finish the wire-wrapped tube bead as desired. Some choices include: leaving the ends as they are; flaring the ends; soldering on flat, concave, or convex end caps; or drilling holes across the diameter of the tube so that it can be strung vertically.

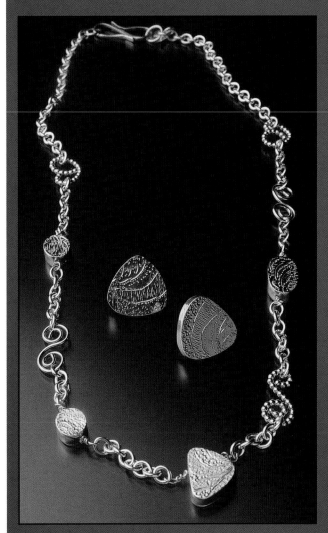

BETTY WHOLEY
Tri Gem, 2004
Necklace, 45 x 15 x 5 cm
Sterling silver and 22-karat gold bi-metal;
fabricated, chased, matted
PHOTO © ARTIST

THE RESHAPED TUBE BEAD

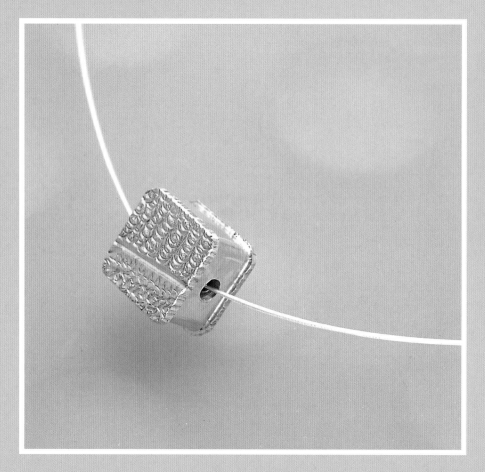

These beads are made from round tubing that has a large outside diameter of 3/8 inch (1 cm) or more. The tubing is made square, round, or triangular on bezel mandrels and becomes the sides of the beads. Sheet metal that has been decorated through roll printing, chasing, stamping, or piercing is then soldered to the ends. This elegant bead is especially attractive when mixed metal ends are applied.

MATERIALS

Seamless tubing, metal of your choice, medium wall, ⅜ inch (1 cm) in diameter or larger

Sheet metal of your choice, 22 gauge or thicker, textured with rolling mill or chasing, stamping, or matting tools if desired

TOOLS & SUPPLIES

Tube jig or dividers
Small tube cutter (optional, available at hardware stores)
Jeweler's saw and saw blades
Saw blade lubricant, beeswax or oil
Soldering kit, page 31
Assorted bezel mandrels
Rawhide mallet or planishing hammer
Sandpaper on sanding stick, 400 grit
Permanent marker
Center punch
Chasing hammer
Drill bits
Flexible shaft machine or hand drill
Scribe
Flat hand file, #2 cut
Scrap wire
Finishing kit, page 40 (optional)

Tip

● Hollow forms trap liquids, such as pickle and water, so be certain they are completely dry before using files on them.

Square bezel mandrel *(left)*, round bezel mandrel *(right)*

STEP BY STEP

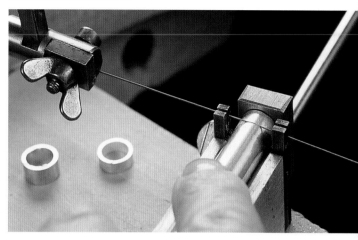

1. Determine the desired width for the sides of the beads. One factor influencing your decision may be the thickness of the cord or chain that will pass through the bead. A good width is ³⁄₁₆ to ⅜ inch (4.8 mm to 1 cm). Adjust the tube cutting jig or dividers to the chosen measurement. Place the tubing in the jig and cut as many lengths as desired (see photo). If using dividers or a small tube cutter, mark the measurement on the tubing with dividers, and then saw off the lengths with a jeweler's saw or a tube cutter.

2. Anneal the cut lengths of tubing. Quench, pickle, and dry them.

3. Place one piece of tubing on the bezel mandrel of your choice. Gently tap each side of the tube against the bezel mandrel with a rawhide mallet (see photo). Eventually, as you pull the tube further onto the mandrel, the tube will conform to its shape. Repeat this step to form the remaining tube lengths.

4. Sand the top and bottom edges of the tubing sections smooth and even. When the tubing is sitting on a hard flat surface, no light should pass through the sanded edge.

5. With a permanent marker, mark two dots on opposite sides of each piece of tubing. These will be where you drill holes for hanging. Place each tubing piece on a bezel mandrel and center punch each mark. Remove the tube from the mandrel and drill the holes. (The holes also allow gases to escape during soldering.)

6. Place one end of a piece of tubing on the plain side of the sheet metal. Trace around the end of the tubing onto the sheet metal. Saw out the sheet metal around the outside of the traced line. (A bit of extra metal around the edge of the tube enables better soldering. It will be trimmed off later.)

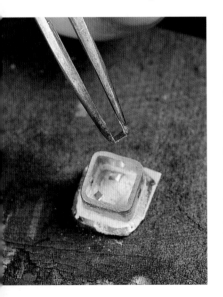

7. Place the sawed-out sheet metal piece on a soldering block with the decorated side down. Flux the piece. Place a piece of the shaped tubing on top of the fluxed sheet. Cut four paillons of hard solder and position them inside the tube, touching the tube and resting on sheet as shown.

8. Light the torch, and heat the piece by tracing the perimeter of the sheet. Keep the tip of the blue cone approximately ¼ inch (6 mm) above the surface of the metal. Remove the heat as soon as you see the solder flow around the edge of the tube.

9. Repeats steps 6–8 for the other pieces of tubing. Quench them in water, and then pickle, rinse, and dry. After this step, one side of each tube bead will be soldered on.

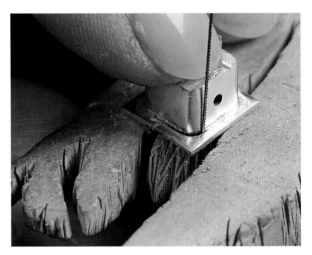

10. Use the jeweler's saw to saw off the excess sheet metal from around the outside of each piece of tubing (see photo). File and sand the cut ends smooth.

11. Repeat steps 6–8 for the other ends of each tube bead, using medium solder. (This closes the other end of the tube and creates the bead.) Quench, pickle, rinse, and dry each bead. Saw off the excess sheet metal on the outside of the tubing, and file and sand the cut edges.

12. If desired, string the beads on a short wire and buff them.

Pauline Warg *Necklace* (detail), 2004. Necklace, 5½ inches (14 cm) in diameter; beads, ½ x ½ inch (1.3 x 1.3 cm). Sugalite, sterling silver, 22-karat gold; chased, stamped, fabricated. Photo by Stewart O'Shields

MAKING SOLDERED DOUBLE-DOME BEADS

The soldered double-dome bead is the quintessential handmade bead. There are dozens of ways to create unique round beads using this technique as the basis of construction, and a multitude of variations are possible. Making a necklace of soldered double-dome beads may be labor-intensive, but it is worth every minute—the result is rewarding and beautiful. It is also an excellent way to hone your soldering skills.

Pauline Warg *Bracelet*, 2003. Bracelet, 7 inches (17.8 cm) long; bead, ½ x ⅜ inch (1.3 x 2 cm). Sterling silver, 24-karat gold; roll printed, kum boo, handmade chain. Photo by Stewart O'Shields

THE DOUBLE-DOME BEAD WITH CENTERED HOLES

Stringing this bead through the center allows both of its sides to be seen. A bead with a center hole can be attractive as a single jewelry element or several can be strung and they can be enjoyed as a group.

MATERIALS

Nonferrous sheet metal of your choice,
    20 to 18 gauge

TOOLS & SUPPLIES

Dividers or plastic circle template
Scribe
Steel block
Center punch
Chasing hammer
Jeweler's saw and 2/0 saw blades
Beeswax or blade lubricant
Soldering kit, page 31
Steel or wood dapping block and punches
Utility hammer or weighted mallet
Sandpaper, 400 grit
Flexible shaft machine or hand drill
Drill bits

STEP BY STEP

1. Using dividers or a circle template and scribe, draw two identical circles onto the 20- or 18-gauge sheet metal. [For this exercise, a circle with a diameter between ½ and 1 inch (1.3 and 2.5 cm) works best.] Mark the center of each circle, and center punch each marked point.

2. Use a jeweler's saw to saw out the two metal disks. Don't file the edges unless there are major irregularities.

3. Anneal the metal disks and quench them in water. Pickle, rinse, and dry the disks.

4. Place one of the disks in the recess of a dapping block. The disk must fit into the recess completely.

5. Choose a dapping punch with a diameter slightly smaller than the diameter of the recess and place it over the metal disk. Using a utility hammer or weighted mallet, firmly and repeatedly tap the end of the punch. Stop tapping when the disk conforms to the recess. Repeat this process with the second disk. Now you have two identically rounded metal domes.

6. If you want to create deeper metal domes, move the disks to recesses that are progressively smaller in diameter (see photo). The dome must always fit into the recess completely. The diameter of the dome will decrease as its depth increases. If you place the dome in a recess that is too small and its edges protrude above the surface of the block, you will cause deep scarring on the metal.

7. Place a piece of 400-grit sandpaper on a flat surface. Put one metal dome on the sandpaper with the rim down. Move the dome back and forth on the sandpaper until the rim is smooth, flat, and even. Repeat this process to sand the rim of the second dome.

8. Drill a small hole in the center of each dome where it has been center punched. These will be the stringing holes on the finished bead. (Always

have an air escape hole in any hollow form before soldering. The expansion of gases during soldering can cause explosions.)

9. Use a knife or a scribe to carve out a shallow recess in a charcoal block. This will keep the metal domes in place during soldering.

10. Place one metal dome in the carved recess on the charcoal block with the drilled hole facing down. Light the torch and warm the dome. Lightly flux the rim of the dome. Cut four paillons of solder, each approximately ¹⁄₁₆-inch (1.6 mm) square. Dip each piece of solder in the flux, and then place them equal distances apart on the rim of the dome. Warm the edge of the dome to dry the flux and to secure the solder to the rim (see photo).

11. Flux the rim of the second metal dome. Using tweezers, pick up the second dome and place it on top of the pieces of solder resting on the rim of the first dome as shown. Be careful to line up the rims as you set down the second dome.

12. Light the torch and evenly heat the bottom dome. The heat will rise to the top dome. Stop heating when the solder flows and the top dome sinks down onto the bottom dome. Turn off the torch.

13. Let the bead cool slightly (approximately 30 seconds). Quench the bead in water, and then place the bead in the pickle. Remove the bead when it is clean of flux, and then rinse and dry it. (The bead may retain some liquid inside. It is a good idea to use a hair dryer to blow air through the holes and dry the bead. Residual moisture can drip on files and other tools and damage them.)

Tips

- If you have problems balancing the top dome on the bottom dome, here are three hints that may be helpful.

  Make certain the pieces of solder are flat and are wider than the rim of the dome.

  Run a length of brass wire through the center hole of the bottom dome, and dig it into the charcoal block. Slip the top dome onto the wire to hold it in place during soldering.

  Alter the process in step 10 as follows: Melt the solder on the edge of the first dome; pickle, rinse, and dry the dome; sand the bumps of solder flat; and then proceed with the instructions.

- If you plan to form beads from mixed-metal sheet, be certain to use hard solder to join the metals on the sheet, and medium or easy solder to join the domes. You then can make the beads using mixed metal in the same way you would use plain or textured sheet metal.

THE DOUBLE-DOME BEAD WITH HOLES THROUGH THE RIM

Beads strung through holes on the rim have many

design possibilities since the full surface of the

dome can be viewed in its entirety. Also, the bead

can easily be reversed to display a different design.

MATERIALS

Nonferrous sheet metal of your choice,
    20 to 18 gauge

TOOLS & SUPPLIES

Dividers or plastic circle template
Scribe
Jeweler's saw and saw blades, 2/0
Beeswax or blade lubricant
Circle-dividing template, page 148
Soldering kit, page 31
Steel or wood dapping block and punches
    or dent-removing block
Utility hammer or weighted mallet
Sandpaper, 400 grit
Round needle file
Cone reamer, 1/10 inch (2.5 mm) in diameter or larger
Flexible shaft machine

STEP BY STEP

1. Using dividers or a circle template and a scribe, draw two identical circles onto the 20- to 18-gauge sheet metal. For this exercise, a circle with a diameter between ½ and 1 inch (1.3 and 2.5 cm) works best.

2. Use the jeweler's saw to saw out the two marked circles. Don't bother to file the edges unless there are major irregularities.

3. To dome the metal disks, follow steps 3–7 of The Double-Dome Bead with Centered Holes on page 104.

4. Center one metal dome on a circle-dividing template (photo A). Use a scribe to make two small marks on the edge of the dome that are 180 degrees apart (photo B).

5. Using a round needle file, begin to file a groove in the rim of the metal dome at the small scribe mark (see photo). This groove creates a half-round channel on the edge of the rim. File another half-round channel at the scribe mark on the opposite side of the same dome. If you hold the two domes together rim to rim, you should be able to see through the seam via the two channels on the rim of one dome.

6. Use a knife or a scribe to carve a shallow recess in a charcoal block. This will keep the metal domes in place during soldering.

7. Place one metal dome in the carved recess on the charcoal block with its round side facing down. Light the torch and warm the dome. Apply a light coat of flux to the rim of the dome. Cut four paillons of solder, each approximately 1/16 inch (1.6 mm) square. Dip each piece of solder in the flux, and then place them on the rim of the dome at equal distances. Do not put any solder in the grooves. Warm the edge of the dome to dry the flux and secure the solder.

8. Flux the rim of the second metal dome. Using tweezers, pick up the second dome and place it on top of the pieces of solder resting on the rim of the first dome. Be careful to line up the rims as you set down the second dome. (Refer to page 106 for tips and options for soldering the domes.)

9. Light the torch and evenly heat the bottom dome. The heat will rise to the top dome. Stop heating when the solder flows and the top dome sinks down onto the bottom dome.

10. Let the bead cool slightly (approximately 30 seconds). Quench the bead in water, and then place it in the pickle. Remove the bead when it is clean of flux, and rinse and dry it. (The bead may retain some liquid inside. It is a good idea to use a hair dryer to blow air through the holes and dry the bead. Residual moisture can drip on files and other tools and damage them.)

12. Attach a cone reamer to the flexible shaft machine and apply a small amount of beeswax to its tip. Place the tip of the cone reamer into one filed opening in the bead (see photo). Hold the reamer vertically into the opening and hold the bead firmly on a table surface. (The other opening in the bead is on the table.) Run the flexible shaft at a slow speed until the reamer widens and rounds out the hole in the bead to the desired size. Repeat this step on the second filed opening.

11. Rest a round needle file in one of the channels in the seam of the bead. Slowly and steadily file across the soldered seam as shown, creating a symmetrical channel in the adjacent dome. Repeat this step on the opposite side of the bead.

EMBELLISHING DOUBLE-DOME BEADS

The double-dome bead is especially interesting and attractive if the surface of the sheet metal is textured or decorated. Depending on the texturing method, some of the work must be done before the domes are fabricated to maintain symmetry. Other decorative surface treatments and textures need to happen at different intervals. These decorating techniques are described in The Basics section of this book. Specific information on when to use them in the process of making soldered double-dome beads is discussed here.

CHASING, STAMPING, MATTING & ROLL PRINTING

1. Clean and anneal a piece of sheet metal. (If roll printing the metal, select a gauge that is thicker than what is needed to form the beads, because roll printing will make the metal thinner.)

2. Texture the sheet metal by chasing, stamping, matting, and/or roll printing.

3. Flatten the textured sheet metal with a rawhide or rubber mallet without scratching or marring the metal.

4. Use dividers or a circle template and a scribe to draw the circles for the dome or domes on the textured sheet metal. (Drawing the circles close, but not touching, will conserve metal.)

5. Fabricate the domed bead following the method described in The Double-Dome Bead with Centered Holes on page 104 or The Double-Dome Bead with Holes through the Soldered Rim on page 107.

PIERCING

1. Use dividers or a circle template with a scribe to draw the circles for the domes onto the sheet metal.

2. Draw or transfer the piercing design onto the metal circles. Scribe over the drawn or transferred design. (This prevents the loss of the design during the forming of the beads.)

3. Use a center punch to dimple the metal at each location where holes need to be drilled for the pierced design. Using a drill bit that makes a hole just large enough for the saw blade to pass through, center punch and drill a hole at each dimple.

4. Anneal the metal, and then form the domes for the beads. (For instructions on doming the metal circles, refer to steps 4–7 on page 105.)

5. Use the jeweler's saw to saw out the pierced design on both metal domes. (All piercing must be done after the domes are formed to maintain the shape of the domes. If the metal is pierced and then domed, the domes will be distorted.)

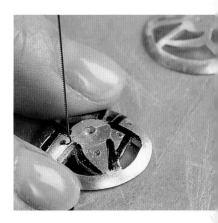

6. Fabricate the domed bead following the method described in The Double-Dome Bead with Centered Holes on page 104 or The Double-Dome Bead with Holes through the Soldered Rim on page 107.

DRILLING DECORATIVE HOLES

1. Use dividers or a circle template with a scribe to draw the circles for the domes onto the sheet metal. With a permanent marker, mark dots on the metal where you want to drill the decorative holes.

2. If the design calls for small drilled holes (18 gauge or Brown & Sharpe 60), you can drill the holes before the domes are formed. If the design calls for larger holes, drill small holes first, form the domes, and then re-drill the holes with a larger drill bit.

3. Fabricate the domed bead following the method described in The Double-Dome Bead with Centered Holes on page 104 or The Double-Dome Bead with Holes through the Soldered Rim on page 107.

TEXTURING THE EDGES WITH A HAMMER

1. Begin with a complete, double-dome bead. Any excess solder or scratches should be sanded off the bead, and the final finish should be on the bead.

2. Place the bead on a firm wood surface and adjust the bead to rest on its soldered edge.

3. Using a cross peen or riveting hammer (a small steel hammer with a narrow face), gently and repeatedly tap the soldered seam of the double-dome bead. Rotate the bead as you hammer, continuing to tap the seam until it is fully textured.

Above: **Pauline Warg** *Earrings*, 1979. Each, ½ x 1¼ inches (1.3 x 3.2 cm) in diameter. Sterling silver; pierced, fabricated. Photo by Stewart O'Shields

Left: **Pauline Warg** *Necklace* (detail), 2002. Necklace, 5½ inches (14 cm) in diameter; each bead, ½ x ⅜ inch (1.3 x 1 cm). Sterling silver, 18-karat gold, 22-karat gold; chased, stamped, roll printed, reticulated, fabricated. Photo by Stewart O'Shields

Making Soldered Double-Dome Beads   113

MAKING .
FUSED BEADS

Most nonferrous metals can be fused or joined without the use of
solder. Pieces of clean metal are placed on top of each other or
crossed over each other, and then the metal is heated carefully. Only
the outer surfaces of the metal pieces melt and flow together, causing
a fused bond. Silver fuses easily, and gold and silver fuse more
strongly and more evenly than copper, brass, or bronze. Fusing can
create interesting textures and shapes and is a great way to use
leftover scraps of wire and sheet.

Left: **Pauline Warg** *Necklace*, 2005. Necklace, 5 inches (12.7 cm) in diameter; bead, 1⁵⁄₁₆ x ⁵⁄₈ inch (3.3 cm x 1.6 cm). Sterling silver, handwoven chain; reticulated, fabricated. Photo by Stewart O'Shields

THE ROUND OR SAUCER-SHAPED FUSED BEAD

Every fused bead is a completely unique creation. When fashioned into round or saucer shapes, they are visually intricate and satisfying.

MATERIALS

Sterling silver wire, 20 gauge, 42 inches (1.1 m)
Sterling silver tubing or jump rings for stringing
(optional)

TOOLS & SUPPLIES

Permanent marker, fine point
Wire clippers
Soldering kit, page 31
Plastic circle template
Dapping block and punches
Utility hammer or weighted mallet
Round-nose pliers

STEP BY STEP

1. Measure 1¼ inches (3.2 cm) of the 20-gauge wire, mark this point with a permanent marker, and then clip the wire on the mark. Hold the cut wire next to the remaining wire, line up the ends, and clip another 1¼-inch (3.2 cm) wire length. Continue to clip matching lengths of wire until you have cut 32 pieces. Do not file or sand the cut wire ends. Cut the remaining wire into ⅜-inch (1 cm) lengths.

2. Place eight of the 1¼-inch (3.2 cm) wire lengths on a flat soldering block. (I prefer to use a jeweler's charcoal block, although other types will work as long as they are flat.) The wire pieces should be evenly spaced,

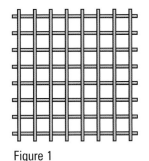

Figure 1

covering an area of 1¼ x 1¼ inches (3.2 x 3.2 cm). Place eight more 1¼-inch (3.2 cm) pieces of wire over the first eight pieces at right angles, forming a square grid of wires (figure 1).

3. Light the torch and adjust the flame to a small non-oxidizing flame. Heat the wire grid evenly until the metal begins to darken. Carefully work the flame over small areas as shown, watching for the metal to appear red, and then very shiny like mercury. The moment you see the surface become shiny, watch for the intersecting wires to flow together. Quickly move the flame to another area and fuse the intersections of wire. (You can return the torch to an area and melt it further as needed.) Be very careful not to let the wires melt too much. It is very easy to melt holes in the grid or large areas into one large mass. Be especially careful near the outer edges of the grid.

4. Repeat steps 2 and 3 with the remaining 16 pieces of 1¼-inch-long (3.2 cm) wire, and then turn off the torch.

5. Quench the two fused-wire squares in water. Pickle, rinse, and dry them.

6. Place the two fused-wire squares on a flat surface. Find a 1⅛-inch (2.9 cm) circle on a plastic template, and center it over one of the wire squares. Using a permanent marker, trace the 1⅛-inch (2.9 cm) circle on the wires. Repeat this step with the second fused-wire square.

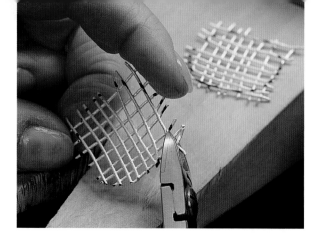

7. Use wire clippers to cut out the circles marked in step 6. This creates two fused-wire circles. Some spaces on the perimeter of the circle will be much larger than others; this is nothing to be concerned about.

8. Find the recess in the dapping block that is closest to 1¼ inches (3.2 cm) in diameter and place one of the fused-wire circles in it. Using a dapping punch that fits the recess, slowly tap the end of the punch with a hammer until the fused-wire piece conforms to the recess. Repeat this process on the second fused-wire circle.

9. Anneal both fused-wire pieces, and then quench them in water. Pickle, rinse, and dry them.

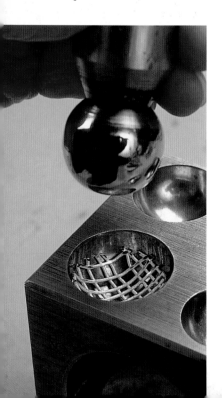

10. Put one of the fused-wire pieces into a smaller recess on the dapping block. Make certain the piece fits into the recess completely. Using a dapping punch that fits the recess, slowly tap the end of the punch with a hammer until the fused-wire piece conforms to the recess as shown. Repeat with the second fused-wire piece. To make the fused pieces deeper,

repeat this step with progressively smaller recesses and progressively smaller punches. You should now have two fused-wire domes with irregular edges.

11. Use round-nose pliers to bend the ⅜-inch (1 cm) lengths of 20-gauge wire into shallow U shapes.

12. Hold the edges of the two fused-wire domes together to resemble a round or saucer-shaped bead. Adjust the domes as needed to get the best fit, and then place them on a soldering block with their edges perpendicular to the surface of the block (see photo). To keep the halves from separating, support the domes with carborundum grain or pieces of pea pumice.

13. Place one of the U-shaped wires over the top of both domes where their edges meet. The ends of the U shape should be resting next to a wire on each dome. Do not wrap the ends of the U-shaped wire into the domes.

14. Light the torch and adjust the flame to a small reducing flame. Fuse one end of the U-shaped wire to each side of the bead, securing the two domes together.

15. Using tweezers, rotate the bead approximately ½ inch (1.3 cm). Fuse another U-shaped wire across the two domes where they meet. Continue fusing short wires to connect the two halves of the bead. There should be a total of five U-shaped wire connectors securing the domes. More wires may be added once the domes are secured.

16. Initially, a chain or cord will not move smoothly through the fused bead. Fortunately, there are two ways to remedy this. Option A: Measure the diameter of the bead and cut a length of tubing equal to or slightly longer than this measurement. (As shown in photo A, the ends of the tube can be flared to keep it in place.) Option B: Solder two jump rings on opposite sides of the bead, and then drill out any wire under the rings, leaving two smooth circles for a cord or chain to pass through (photo B).

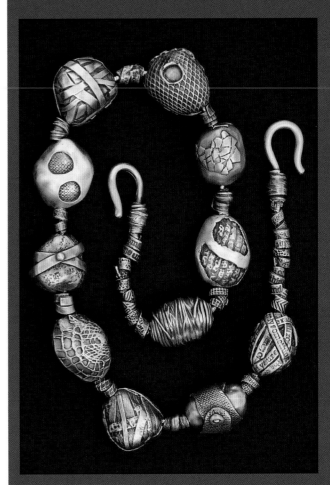

HADAR JACOBSON
Eleven Rocks, 2004
45 cm
Metal clay; hollow formed, textured, fired, oxidized
PHOTO © ARTIST

THE TUBULAR FUSED BEAD

To create this intriguing bead, you will lay out a grid of rectangular wire, fuse the seams, and then form it into a cylinder. You can close the ends with caps as shown, or simply leave the wire free.

MATERIALS

Sterling silver wire, 20 gauge, 10 pieces,
   each 2 inches (5.1 cm) long
Sterling silver wire, 20 gauge, 12 pieces,
   each 1½ inches (3.8 cm) long
Sterling silver sheet, 18 gauge, ¾ x 1½ inches
   (1.9 x 3.8 cm)

TOOLS & SUPPLIES

Soldering kit, page 31
Half-round/flat pliers
Wood dowel, ⅜ inch (9.5 mm) in diameter
Wood ring-bending block or sandbag
Rawhide or plastic mallet
Permanent marker or scribe
Plastic circle template
Jeweler's saw frame and saw blades, 2/0
Beeswax or blade lubricant
Flat file, #2 cut
Sanding stick, 400 grit
Steel block
Center punch
Chasing hammer
Flexible shaft machine or hand drill
Drill bit, #60 (1.02 mm)

STEP BY STEP

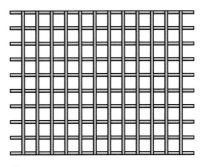

Figure 1

1. Position the 2-inch-long (5.1 cm) wires on a
flat soldering block horizontally and align their
ends. As shown in figure 1, space the wires to form
a rectangle that is 2 x 1½ inches (5.1 x 3.8 cm).

Figure 2

2. Starting ⅛ inch (3 mm) from both ends of the
2-inch (5.1 cm) wires, place the 1½-inch-long
(3.8 cm) wires on top of and perpendicular to the
2-inch (5.1 cm) wires, forming a grid as shown
in figure 2.

3. Light the torch and adjust the flame to a small
reducing flame. Heat the entire rectangular grid of
wires until they become dark gray to light red.
Focus the flame on one small area at a time until
the wires are red, and then very shiny silver, like
mercury. Keep the flame moving in that area until
you can see the intersecting wires flow together on
the surface, and then move the flame to another
area until the whole grid is fused at every intersecting wire. Turn off the torch.

4. Quench the fused wire grid in water. Pickle,
rinse, and dry it.

5. Using the
rounded side of
the half-round/flat
pliers, begin to
bend the fused
grid into a cylinder
or a tube. Start the
bend from the
ends of the 2-inch
(5.1 cm) wires.

6. Place the dowel inside the fused wire piece. Put both pieces into a recess on the ring-bending block or on the sandbag. Using a mallet, tap the fused wire piece over the dowel to make it more evenly cylindrical (see photo). As the cylinder becomes smaller, let the wire ends cross over each other. (They will resemble Xs on the connecting edge.) Bend these end wires down over each other so they overlap, and make certain they are touching. (This flattens the X shapes so the form is more evenly tubular or cylindrical.)

Tips

- Fused metal is brittle, so take care when bending or forming it.

- Some metalsmiths prefer to flux all the metal before fusing. If you choose to do so, be frugal. Too much flux will make the wires move around and can inhibit your ability to see the fusion.

7. Light the torch and adjust the flame for fusing (a small reducing flame). Set the cylinder on a soldering block with the overlapping wires facing up. Move the flame over the overlapping wires until they fuse, securing and completing the cylinder (see photo). Quench the cylinder in water. Pickle, rinse, and dry.

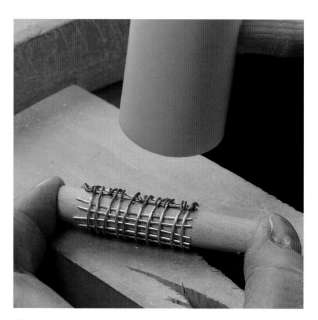

8. Place the dowel into the cylinder and tap it with a mallet until the shape is even.

9. Measure the diameter of both ends of the cylinder and add ⅛ inch (3 mm) to these measurements. Use a permanent marker or scribe to trace two circles onto the sheet silver that correspond to the measurements. Mark the center of both circles.

10. Use a jeweler's saw to cut out the two marked circles. Smooth their edges with a file or sandpaper. Center punch and drill the marked center point of each circle.

11. File or sand the ends of the cylinder to make them more even. When placed on end on a level surface, the cylinder must have four or more spots touching it evenly.

12. Place one of the silver disks on a soldering block. Flux the disk and the matching end of the cylinder. Place the cylinder, fluxed end down, onto the disk. Cut a small paillon of medium silver solder for each contact point between the cylinder and the disk. Use soldering tweezers to place one piece of solder next to each contact point.

13. Light the torch and adjust the flame to a reducing flame with an inner blue cone that is as long as the diameter of the cylinder. Point the cone toward the disk and evenly heat the entire piece until all the solder flows. (Since the wires are much smaller than the disk, it is easy to overheat the wires and not have the solder flow.) Repeat steps 13 and 14 with the second disk and the opposite end of the cylinder. Quench the bead in water. Pickle, rinse, and dry.

14. Depending on the diameter of the cord or chain on which you want to hang the bead, you may need to redrill the holes in the disks to enlarge them.

Variations
• Use pieces of scrap silver in place of the wires, but be sure to evenly space the scrap to equalize the stress when forming.
• Create different patterns by placing the wires unevenly or not at right angles.
• Fuse additional wires to the fused grid.
• Once the wires are fused, run the grid through a rolling mill to flatten it.
• Fused beads look very nice when oxidized and then buffed lightly to create highlights.

AARON F. MACSAI
Pattern Play, 2005
14- and 18-karat yellow and pink gold, sterling silver, copper; extruded, milled, soldered, forged, filed, etched, oxidized
PHOTO © ARTIST

Pauline Warg *Necklace* (detail), 2005.
Necklace, 5½ inches (14 cm) in diameter;
each bead, 1¾ x ⅝ x ½ inch (4.4 x 1.6 x 1.3 cm),
Sterling silver, blister pearl, pearls; roll printed, hydraulic
press formed, fabricated. Photo by Stewart O'Shields

MAKING BEADS

WITH THE

HYDRAULIC PRESS

The hydraulic press is a tool that can form and stretch metal in many unique ways. In this section, I will explain two very different methods for using the hydraulic press to help create metal bead forms. Although many types of hydraulic presses are available, these projects were made using a 20-ton hand-pumped hydraulic press with a pressure gauge. Forming metal with the hydraulic press does not destroy surface decoration. Roll printed, etched, chased, or matted sheet metal will work very well for these beads, as will mixed-metal sheets.

THE MATRIX DIE-FORMED BEAD

A matrix is a sheet of rigid acrylic out of which a pattern has been pierced. The hydraulic press is used to press sheet metal into this cutout pattern, yielding a dimensional form. Beads made with this technique can have softly flowing organic shapes (below, left), geometric contours (below, right), and limitless outlines in between.

MATERIALS

Acrylite plastic sheet, 3 x 3 x ¼ inch
 (7.6 x 7.6 x 0.6 cm)*
Sterling silver sheet, 20 gauge, 3 x 1 inch
 (7.6 x 2.5 cm)
Urethane sheet, 80 durometer, ¹⁄₁₆ or ⅛ inch
 (1.6 or 3 mm) thick

TOOLS & SUPPLIES

Glue stick
Permanent marker, fine point
Flexible shaft machine or hand drill
Drill bit, #60 (1.02 mm)
Jeweler's saw blades for plastic or wax cutting
Jeweler's saw frame
Beeswax or synthetic lubricant
Saw block
Half-round hand file, #2
Soldering kit, page 31
Jeweler's saw blades, 2/0
Hydraulic press, 20 ton, with gauge
Sandpaper, 400 grit
Finishing kit, page 40

*Acrylite is a sheet plastic that does not contain
formaldehyde, which can gas out during sawing and
form fumes that are toxic to some people.

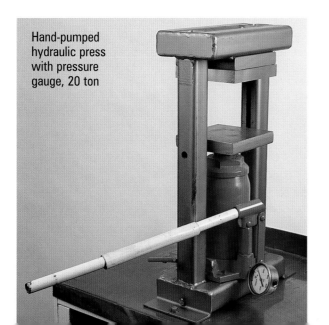

Hand-pumped
hydraulic press
with pressure
gauge, 20 ton

STEP BY STEP

1. Design and draw on paper a simple shape that
is no larger than 1 inch (2.5 cm) long x ⁵⁄₁₆ inch
(7.9 mm) wide. Shapes that will work include a
square, rectangle, oval, marquis, or simple variations
of these. Don't design a shape with a lot of narrow
points. Cut out the shape with scissors, and then
use the glue stick to adhere it to the center of the
Acrylite sheet. Rub out any air bubbles under the
paper, and let the glue dry.

2. Trace the
perimeter of the
cut paper onto
the Acrylite sheet
with a pencil or
permanent
marker. (This
prevents the
design from being
lost should the
paper peel off
during sawing.) Drill a hole through the Acrylite
sheet that is ⅛ inch (3 mm) inside one of the edges
of the cut-paper design (see photo).

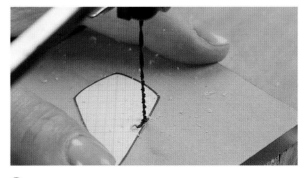

3. Feed a plastic- or wax-cutting saw blade through
the hole in the Acrylite and tighten the blade in the
saw frame. Put a small amount of lubricant on the
blade. Rest the Acrylite sheet flat on a bench pin
and saw out the design shape as shown.

(Sawing Acrylite can be slow and messy. The dust has static electricity and sticks to everything.) Remove the blade, and then use a half-round hand file to smooth the inside edges of the Acrylite. File a very slight bevel on the top and bottom edges of the cutout.

4. Place the Acrylite sheet over the sheet of 80-durometer urethane. Trace the cut-out design onto the urethane with a permanent marker. Repeat this process two more times, drawing a total of three shapes. Use scissors to cut the shapes out of the urethane.

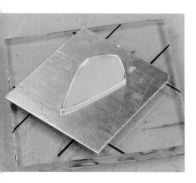

5. Draw lines with a permanent marker along the furthest points of the width and length extending beyond and intersecting on to the plastic (see photo). These lines will act as a guide to center the metal during pressing.

6. Anneal the 20-gauge silver sheet, and then quench it in water. Pickle, rinse, and dry it. Saw the sheet in half lengthwise, creating two 1½ x 1-inch (3.8 x 2.5 cm) pieces.

7. Center one of the metal pieces on the Acrylite sheet, using the marker lines as a guide. Center one of the urethane cutouts on top of the metal. Place the stacked Acrylite, metal, and urethane in the center of the lower platen of the hydraulic press. (The Acrylite should be on the bottom of the stack.) Be careful not to jostle the pieces out of alignment.

8. Pump the hydraulic press until the urethane makes contact with the upper platen. Continue to pump until there is no space visible between the metal and the upper platen (photo A). Release the pressure. When the platen is lowered far enough to remove the three layers, close the valve. The metal should now have a slight impression of the cut-out design (photo B).

9. Repeat steps 7 and 8 with the second 1½ x 1-inch (3.8 x 2.5 cm) metal piece. If you are working with an asymmetrical design, flip over the Acrylite and press the second metal piece from the opposite side to create a mirror image.

10. Anneal the two pressed metal pieces, and then quench them in water. Pickle, rinse, and dry them.

11. Place one of the pressed metal pieces over the cutout in the Acrylite sheet, lining up the impression in the metal with the cutout. Place all three of the

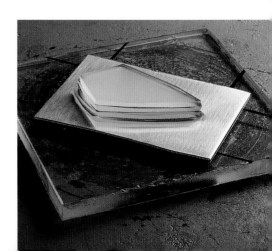

urethane pieces on top of the impression (see photo). Carefully place the Acrylite, metal, and urethane in the center of the lower platen of the hydraulic press. (The Acrylite should be on the bottom of the stack.)

12. Slowly pump the hydraulic press until the pressure gauge reads 2,000 PSI (pounds per square inch). Hold the pressure at 2,000 PSI for 30 seconds, and then release the pressure. Lower the platen, and then tighten the valve.

13. Repeat steps 11 and 12 with the second piece of pressed metal. If an asymmetrical shape, see step 9.

14. On the top side of each pressed metal piece there is a line created by the edge of the Acrylite that defines the perimeter of the design. Trace over this line with a permanent marker on both metal pieces. Saw out each pressed metal shape along the marked line. Now you have two recessed shapes that fit together to make a hollow form (see photo). After sawing, do not sand or file the edges too close to the marked line. (That will be done after soldering.)

15. Place a piece of 400-grit sandpaper on a firm, flat surface. With its concave side towards the sandpaper, move one pressed metal piece back and forth to create a flat even edge. Repeat with the second piece of pressed metal. When held together, the edges of the metal pieces should meet flatly and evenly.

16. Before soldering the two pressed metal pieces together, drill a hole in one or both halves to allow gases to escape while heating. Or, instead of drilling a hole or holes, file a notch on the edge of one or both metal pieces. (The drilled holes could later be used for hanging the finished bead.)

17. Place the two pressed metal pieces on a soldering block with their concave sides facing up. Apply flux to the edges of the forms. Cut six pieces of medium solder, each 1/16 inch (1.6 mm) square. Evenly space the solder on the edge of one pressed metal piece.

18. Light the torch and adjust the flame to a slightly oxidizing flame with a blue cone that is approximately 1/2 inch (1.3 cm) long. (When soldering hollow forms, more heat is needed than when soldering flat sheet.) Warm the pressed metal piece with the solder resting on it until the flux dries and the solder is stuck on, but does not flow.

19. Pick up the second pressed metal piece with soldering tweezers and carefully place it on the piece with solder on its edges. Adjust the placement as needed so the two halves line up evenly on top of each other. Pointing the flame at the bottom metal piece, begin to heat the pieces evenly. Move the flame around the forms until the top form sinks down onto the bottom form. You should see the solder flow around the touching edges. Remove the heat.

20. Let the bead air cool for a minute, and then quench it in water. (Hot, hollow forms will become vacuums if quenched hot.) Pickle, rinse, and dry the bead. If there is liquid inside the bead, place it on a paper towel. The towel should siphon out some of the liquid. A hair dryer can also be used to warm and dry the bead.

21. File or sand the edges of the bead to make it smooth and even. Finish the bead as desired.

Making Beads with the Hydraulic Press   **129**

THE PRESSED TUBE BEAD

The form of this type of bead has a spontaneous quality. Rarely
will two of them have similar shapes. The metal stretches and
collapses due to the pressure of the press. In the end, the tubing
looks like a thick liquid being poured.

MATERIALS

Sterling silver tubing, heavy wall thickness
(0.04 inch, 1 mm, 18 gauge), ½ inch (1.3 cm) in
outside diameter

Urethane sheet, 80 durometer, 1 x 6 x ⅛ inch
(2.5 x 15.2 x 0.3 mm)

Sterling silver sheet, 18 gauge, ⅝ x 1½ inches
(1.6 x 3.8 cm)

2 sterling silver jump rings, 16 gauge, ¼ inch (6 mm)
in outside diameter

TOOLS & SUPPLIES

Sandpaper, 400 grit

Dividers

Jeweler's saw frame and saw blades, 2/0

Beeswax or blade lubricant

Permanent marker, fine point

Hydraulic press, 20 ton

Soldering kit, page 31

Flat hand file, #2

Steel block

Center punch

Chasing hammer

Flexible shaft machine

Drill bit, #60

Chain- or flat-nose pliers, 2 pairs

Cone reamer, ¼ inch (6 mm)

STEP BY STEP

1. File the end of the ½-inch (1.3 cm) heavy-walled tubing straight and smooth. Set the legs of the dividers ¾ inch (1.9 cm) apart. Hold one leg against the end of the tubing and scribe a line around the tubing with the other leg.

2. Holding the tubing securely on your bench pin, use the saw to score the tube on the line made by the dividers, and then saw all the way through it. Sand the ends of the cut tubing smooth.

3. Trace the inside diameter of the tube onto the 80-durometer urethane eight times. Use scissors to cut these small circles out of the urethane as shown.

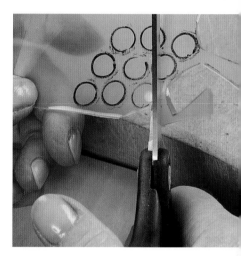

4. Place the ¾-inch (1.9 cm) piece of tubing in the center of the lower platen of the hydraulic press. Stack six pieces of the urethane inside the tube and the remaining two pieces above the end of the tubing (see photo).

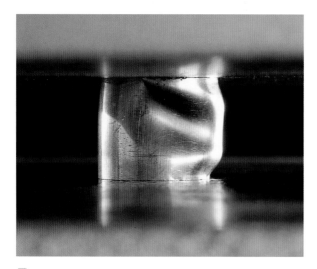

5. Slowly begin to pump the press. When the top piece of urethane touches the top platen, make certain it stays lined up with the inside of the tube. Continue to add pressure. The urethane will compress into the tube. The tube will begin to bulge and distort (see photo). Watch carefully and stop pumping the press when you are pleased with the bulges and crinkles. Release the pressure and let the platen drop. Close the valve.

6. Remove the urethane from inside the tube. Make the ends of the tube smooth and even again. Sometimes the edges roll in or out. You need to sand the ends to create a bit of a flat edge all the way around.

7. Cut the piece of 18-gauge sterling silver sheet in half lengthwise.

8. Place one of the sterling silver pieces on a soldering block. Cut four ¹⁄₁₆-inch (1.6 mm) pieces of hard silver solder. Flux the sheet and one end of the tube, and place the fluxed tube end on the sheet. Put the solder pieces along the inside edge of the tube.

9. Light the torch and adjust the flame until you have a blue cone that is approximately ¾ inch (1.9 cm) long. This should be an oxidizing flame. Point the tip of the blue cone at the sterling silver sheet and rotate the flame around the tube to evenly heat it. Watch for the solder to flow out and around the edge of the tube. Remove the heat and turn off the torch. Quench, pickle, rinse, and dry the piece.

10. Use a jeweler's saw to trim the end cap to the desired size and shape. File the cut edges smooth.

11. Center punch and drill a small hole in the center of the end cap. This hole will act as a gas escape when the other end is soldered. (Also, it will be one of the holes for stringing the finished bead.)

12. Repeat steps 8–11 with the other piece of sterling silver sheet and the open end of the tube. Make sure to drain any water or pickle that is inside the bead.

13. Close both of the sterling silver jump rings. Sand one side of each jump ring slightly flat.

14. Place one end of the bead on a soldering block. Flux the other end of the bead. Place the flat side of one jump ring on the fluxed end of the bead, and center it around the drilled hole.

15. Cut four ¹⁄₁₆-inch (1.6 mm) squares of medium silver solder. Place two of the solder pieces on the interior of the jump ring (see photo).

16. Light the torch and adjust the flame to an oxidizing flame with a blue cone that is ¾ inch (1.9 cm) long. Heat the bead evenly, pointing the tip of the blue cone at the tube. When the solder flows around the jump ring and onto the end cap, remove the heat and turn off the torch.

17. Turn the bead over and repeat steps 14–16. Quench the bead in water, and then pickle, rinse, and dry it.

18. Put the cone reamer in the flexible shaft machine and put a little beeswax on the reamer. Place the tip of the reamer in one of the bead holes. Using a very slow speed, run the reamer and let it shave the hole larger (see photo). Stop when the hole is the desired size. Repeat the process on the other end of the bead.

Variations
• File or grind some lines on the tube before pressing it. The tube will move differently where there are thin spots.
• Etch, chase, or texture the tube before pressing it.
• Use beaded wire to make the jump rings around the end holes.
• Extend the end caps approximately ¹⁄₁₆ inch (1.6 mm) past the diameter of the tube bead.
• Use a narrow-faced hammer to create a chinked texture on the edge of the end cap.

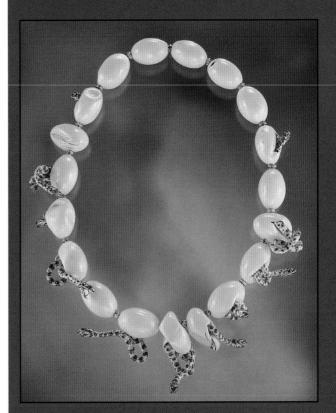

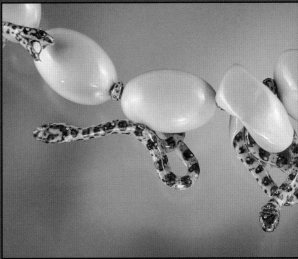

DAVID C. FREDA
Study of Northern Black Rat Snakes
with Eggs Neckpiece, 2005
24.1 x 17.8 x 2.5 cm
Fine silver, 24- and 18-karat yellow gold, enamel; hollow-core cast, fabricated

MAKING MORE
METAL BEADS

Pauline Warg *Necklace* (detail), 2005. 5½ inches (14 cm) in diameter; beads, ¾ x ¾ x ⁵⁄₁₆ inch (1.9 x 1.9 x 0.8 cm) and ⅝ x ⅝ x ⁵⁄₁₆ inch (1.6 x 1.6 x 0.8 cm). Copper, brass, sterling silver, nickel; twisted wire patterned sheet, formed, fabricated Photo by Stewart O'Shields

You will use many of the fabrication skills and decorative techniques you have learned in this book to create the three forms pictured below—The Square Bead (top left), The Crescent Roll Bead (bottom left), and The Eight-Dome Bead (below). These beads are easier to construct than you might imagine, and they respond well to dramatic surface treatments, such as chasing, reticulation, and filigree.

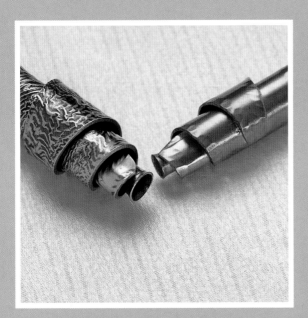

THE SQUARE BEAD

This bead is one of my favorites. It's easy to make and looks very sophisticated. The square bead can be produced with pierced, patterned, or textured metal. It can be created in many different sizes, and it works well for constructing graduated necklaces.

MATERIALS

Sterling silver sheet, 18 gauge, ¾ x 1½ inches (1.9 x 3.2 cm)

Sterling silver tubing, 3 mm in outside diameter, ⅞ inch (2.2 cm) long

TOOLS & SUPPLIES

Steel scribe
Plastic square template (optional)
Jeweler's saw frame and 2/0 saw blades
Beeswax or blade lubricant
Sandpaper, 400 grit
Flat hand file, #2
Wood or metal dapping block and punches
Weighted rawhide mallet
Soldering kit, page 31
Steel bench block
Tapered steel tool or center punch, approximately ⅛ to ¼ inch (3 to 6 mm) in diameter

STEP BY STEP

1. Cut the 18-gauge sterling silver sheet in half lengthwise to make two ¾-inch (1.9 cm) squares. Or, if you have a larger piece of metal, draw two ¾-inch (1.9 cm) squares with a scribe and a square template or ruler and use a jeweler's saw to cut out the two squares. File the edges of the squares smooth and even with a #2 flat hand file, maintaining a good square shape.

2. Dap each of the metal squares in a recess of a dapping block that is 1³⁄₁₆ to 1¼ inches (3 to 3.2 cm) in diameter. The depth in the center of the square should be ⅛ to ¼ inch (3 to 6 mm).

3. Place a piece of 400-grit sandpaper on a hard, flat surface. Hold one of the dapped squares, points down, on the sandpaper. Move the metal square back and forth on the sandpaper as shown until you create flat spots without losing the square corner. Repeat with the second metal square.

4. Place one of the metal squares, concave side facing up, on a soldering block. Flux each of the flat spots on the corners. Cut four pieces of medium silver solder, each ¹⁄₁₆ inch (1.6 mm) square. Place one solder piece on each corner of the metal square.

5. Light the torch and adjust the flame to a soft (reducing) flame with a blue cone that is ¾ inch (1.9 cm) long. Gently heat the metal square on the soldering block until the flux dries, holding the solder in place.

6. Flux the flat corners of the second dapped metal square. Use tweezers to place this square on the one on the soldering block (hot!), carefully lining up the corners.

7. Heat the metal with the torch evenly and completely until the solder flows and the squares are soldered together. Remove the heat and shut off the torch. Quench the bead in water. Pickle, rinse, and dry it.

8. Double-check the sides of the bead. If they don't line up perfectly, sand or file the sides to even them out.

9. Place the bead on one of its sides on a steel block. Place the tip of the tapered tool between the two halves of the bead as shown. Tap the other end of the tapered rod with a mallet. Spread the two halves of the bead with the tool until the opening is ⅛ inch (3 mm) wide in the center. Flip the bead over on the block and repeat this process on the opposite side.

10. Slip the ⅞-inch (2.2 cm) piece of tubing through the side of the bead spread in step 9. Place one of tubing ends on the steel block. Put the narrow end of the tapered rod in the end of the tube. Gently tap the other end of the rod with a mallet. Stop tapping when the end of the tube is slightly flared (see photo). Turn the bead over and flare the other end in the same way.

THE CRESCENT ROLL BEAD

We have the dinner roll to thank for inspiring this versatile bead. Its construction is very simple, and it is easy to form the bead in a variety of sizes. You can create many variations of the crescent roll bead by using patterned, textured, or hammered sheet metal. The foundation of the bead is a triangle. By changing the proportions of the triangle, the effect of the bead changes. The crescent roll bead works best when thinner gauges of sheet metal are used, such as 22 to 26 gauge.

MATERIALS

Sterling silver sheet metal, 24 gauge, 1 x 2 inches
(2.5 x 5.1 cm)
Sterling silver tubing, medium wall, ⁵⁄₃₂ inch (4 mm)
outside diameter

TOOLS & SUPPLIES

Graph paper, 1-inch-square (2.5 cm) grids,
10 sections per inch
Ruler, 6 inches (15.2 cm)
Glue stick
Jeweler's saw frame and 2/0 saw blades
Beeswax or blade lubricant
Flat hand file, #2 cut
Sandpaper, 400 grit
Steel bench block
Narrow-faced (⅛-inch [3 mm]) forging hammer
Soldering kit, page 31
Drill bit, ⅛ inch (3 mm) in diameter
Flat-nose pliers
Ball punch, 5 mm in diameter
Chasing hammer

STEP BY STEP

1. On the graph paper, draw a straight line that is
1 inch (2.5 cm) long (10 squares). Measure
2 inches (5.1 cm) from that line (20 squares). Draw
a second line that is parallel to the first, 2 inches
(5.1 cm) away from it, that starts and ends with the
same squares.

2. Make a small pencil mark on the second line at
its center point (the fifth square). Connect the left
end of the first line with the center point on the
second line. Draw a line from the right end of the
first line to the center point of the second line. You

have drawn an isosceles triangle that has two equal
sides and two equal angles.

3. Cut out the triangle with scissors. Use the glue
stick to glue it to the 1 x 2-inch (2.5 x 5.1 cm)
sterling silver sheet. (The sample sheet is roll
printed.) Using a jeweler's saw, saw out the triangle.
File, and then sand all the cut edges smooth.

4. Place the silver
triangle on the steel
bench block. With
the forging hammer,
lightly hammer all
the way around
the triangle at a
90-degree angle to
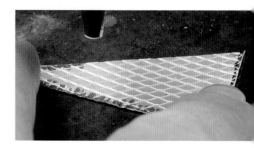
the edge and ⅛ inch (3 mm) inside the edge (see
photo). This creates a decorative edging that helps
accent the form.

5. Measure and saw off 1⅛ inches (2.9 cm) of the
silver tubing. File and sand the ends smooth. Place
the tubing on a flat, clean soldering block.

6. Flux the length of tubing. Cut two pieces of
medium silver solder, each ¹⁄₁₆ inch (1.6 mm)
square. Place the solder squares on top of the

tubing. Flux the 1-inch-long (2.5 cm) side of the silver triangle, with the hammered edge facing up. Carefully place the triangle on top of the solder on top of the tube (see photo).

7. Light the torch and adjust the flame to an oxidizing flame with a ¾-inch (1.9 cm) blue cone. Heat the tube with the triangle on top, until the solder flows and connects them. Quench the piece in water, and then pickle, rinse, and dry it.

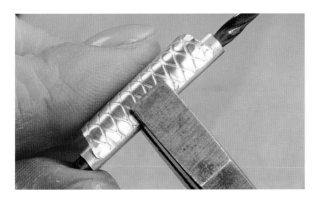

8. Place the drill bit into the piece of tubing. The drill bit should fit snugly. Begin to roll the metal triangle around the tube as shown. If it is difficult to roll, alternate gripping the middle of the tube and sheet, and gripping the end of tube onto the drill bit for more control.

9. As you roll the metal triangle around the tube there should be a slight, even space all the way around. The cross section will resemble a spiral. When the entire triangle is wrapped around the tube, press down the very tip of the triangle to touch the metal under it (see photo).

10. Cut one piece of easy silver solder into a ¹⁄₁₆-inch (1.6 mm) square. Flux the spot where the tip of the triangle touches the metal and wedge the piece of solder under the tip of the bead (see photo). Place the rolled bead on a soldering block with the tip of the triangle facing up.

11. Light the torch and adjust the flame to an oxidizing flame with a ¾-inch-long (1.9 cm) blue cone. Heat the piece evenly until the solder flows, securing the tip of the triangle. Quench the bead in water. Pickle, rinse and dry it.

12. Place one end of the tubing on a steel bench block. Place the ball punch in the other end of the tube, vertically. Tap lightly on the flat end of the punch until the end of the tubing begins to flare (see photo). Repeat this step on the other end of the tube.

Variations

• Roll print, reticulate, chase, stamp, or hammer the sheet-metal triangle before it is formed.

• Use a mixed-metal sheet to make the bead.

• Saw the long edge of the triangle so that it is slightly wavy, not straight.

• Leave the end of the tube straight, rather than flaring it.

• Solder decorative wire (such as twisted, square, or beaded) around the ends of the tubing.

Pauline Warg *Necklace* (detail), 2005. Necklace, 5½ inches (14 cm) in diameter; handmade beads, each 1⅛ x ½ inch (2.9 x 1.3 cm). Sterling silver, freshwater pearls; reticulated, fabricated. Photo by Stewart O'Shields

THE EIGHT-DOME BEAD

The eight-dome folded bead is formed from two main parts, and making it requires some complex sawing. This interesting bead works best as a pendant and can be decorated in a number of ways.

These instructions show you how to lay out, form, and construct the bead. Different decorating options are listed at the end of the instructions. Once you see the bead, you may think of many other ways to embellish it.

MATERIALS

Sterling silver sheet, 22 gauge, 1¾ x 1¾ inches (4.4 x 4.4 cm)

Sterling silver sheet, 22 gauge, 1 x 1 inch (2.5 x 2.5 cm)

Sterling silver round wire, 18 gauge, 2 inches (5.1 cm) long

TOOLS & SUPPLIES

Metal scribe
Plastic circle template
Steel bench block
Center punch
Chasing hammer
Flexible shaft machine or hand drill
Drill bit, 1 mm in diameter
Jeweler's saw frame and saw blades (3/0 or 4/0)
Beeswax or saw blade lubricant
Sandpaper, 400 grit
Half-round file, #2 or #4 cut
Soldering kit, page 31
Wood dapping or dent-removing block and punches
Hemispherical dapping block and punches
Lead forming block (optional)*
Utility hammer or weighted mallet
Round-nose pliers
2 pairs of chain-nose pliers

*A lead forming block (see photo below) is a 3 x 3 x 1-inch (7.6 x 7.6 x 2.5 cm) block of lead available at some hardware or jewelry supply stores. Like pitch, the block allows you to create an impression to fit your needs.

STEP BY STEP

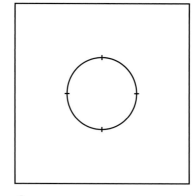

Figure 1

1. Use a scribe and a plastic template to trace a ¾-inch (1.9 cm) circle on the center of the 1¾-inch (4.4 cm) square sterling silver sheet (figure 1). The plastic template will have four division marks (quarters) on the perimeter of the circle. Make a scribe mark on the traced circle at each of the quarter marks as shown.

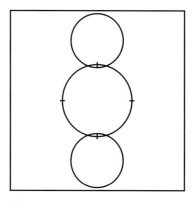

Figure 2

2. Place the ⁹⁄₁₆-inch (1.4 cm) circle of the plastic template so it slightly overlaps the scribed edge of the ¾-inch (1.9 cm) circle at one of the quarter marks. (The overlap should be approximately ¹⁄₃₂ inch [0.8 mm].) Trace the circle. Trace another ⁹⁄₁₆-inch (1.4 cm) circle slightly overlapping the ¾-inch (1.9 cm) circle on the opposite quarter mark. You now have three scribed circles as shown in figure 2.

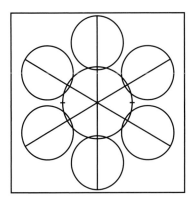

Figure 3

3. With the scribe and the plastic template, trace two more ⁹⁄₁₆-inch (1.4 cm) circles evenly between each of the first two ⁹⁄₁₆-inch (1.4 cm) circles on each side. Slightly overlap the ¾-inch (1.9 cm) circle with these four new circles. There is now one ¾-inch (1.9 cm) circle with six ⁹⁄₁₆-inch (1.4 cm) circles (figure 3).

4. Use a scribe and a plastic template to trace a ⅞-inch (2.2 cm) diameter circle onto the 1-inch (2.5 cm) square of sterling silver sheet. Mark the center of the circle, center punch it, and then drill a 1-mm hole at this point.

5. Using a jeweler's saw, cut out the seven-circle shape on the 1¾ x 1¾-inch (4.4 cm) sterling silver sheet as one piece, and then saw out the ⅞-inch (2.2 cm) circle from the 1-inch (2.5 cm) square sterling silver sheet.

6. Sand the edges of both sawed metal forms smooth. (If there are gross irregularities on the edges, use a file to smooth them before sanding.) Anneal the two metal shapes, and then quench, pickle, and rinse them.

7. Find a ¹⁵⁄₁₆-inch (2.4 cm) recess on the wood dapping block or use a lead forming block as shown. Pick up the larger metal form (the one with seven scribed circles); place one of its scribed circles in the recess, and slightly dome the metal with a wood or a steel dap. Repeat this process to dome each of the remaining scribed circles and to dome the ⅞-inch (2.2 cm) sterling silver circle.

8. Hold the seven-dome metal form with the ¾-inch (1.9 cm) dome on top. Manipulate the six smaller domes so that the right edge of each one is under the left edge of the adjacent one (photo A). Place this metal form into a recess in a steel dapping block that is larger than the form. Choose a dapping punch that fits into the same recess. Place the punch in the partially domed form and tap it into the recess (photo B). Move the metal to a smaller recess and dap again. The seven-dome metal form should now be three-quarters of a sphere.

9. Place one end of the 18-gauge wire in insulated-grip soldering tweezers. Light the torch and adjust the flame to a small oxidizing flame. Hold the other end of the wire directly in front of the tip of the blue cone of the flame. The wire will start to melt and form a ball on the end. When the ball is ¹/₁₄ to ⅛ inch (2 to 3 mm) in diameter, pull the wire away from the flame. Quench the balled wire in water, and then dry it.

10. Feed the wire through the hole in the center of the ⅞-inch (2.2 cm) metal dome with the ball on the concave side of the dome as shown.

13. Cut six ¹/₁₆-inch-square (1.6 x 1.6 mm) pieces of medium silver sheet solder. Place one solder piece in each of the crevices where the domes touch. Light the torch and evenly heat the metal until the solder flows and connects the two pieces (see photo). Quench, pickle, rinse, and dry the bead.

14. Make a 90-degree bend in the 18-gauge wire that is ³/₁₆ inch (4.8 mm) from the point where the wire exits the bead. Gently grip the wire with round-nose pliers ¾ inch (1.9 cm) away from the 90-degree bend. Roll a loop in the wire, leaving approximately 1 inch (2.5 cm) of wire from the end of the loop to the end of the wire.

15. Grip the wire loop sideways in one pair of chain-nose pliers. With the other pair of chain-nose pliers, grip the end of the wire. Gently and evenly wrap the remaining wire tail below the loop as shown until it reaches the top of bead. This creates a loop from which to hang the bead.

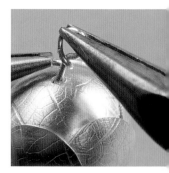

11. Turn the ⅞-inch (2.2 cm) metal dome sideways and slip it into the seven-dome metal form at an angle (see photo). Holding the long end of the wire, straighten the ⅞-inch (2.2 cm) dome into place, evenly set against the tips of the six ⁹/₁₆-inch (1.4 cm) domes.

12. Place the end of the wire in insulated-grip soldering tweezers. (The seven-dome metal shape should be hanging off the edge of the ⅞-inch [2.2 cm] dome.) Apply flux to the points where the ⅞-inch (2.2 cm) dome touches the inside of the ⁹/₁₆-inch (1.4 cm) domes.

Variations
• Roll print all of the metal before laying out the circles.
• Lay out the circles, and then draw a design in each of the shapes for piercing.
• Solder decorative wires and/or small balls onto the domes.
• Solder bezel cups or small bezels onto the domes, and then set stones after all soldering is complete.

Pauline Warg *Necklace* (detail), 2005. Bead, 1⅛ x ⅞ inch (2.9 x 2.2 cm) in diameter.
Sterling silver; roll printed, fabricated, oxidized. Photo by Stewart O'Shields

TEMPLATES & CHARTS

MAKING A
CIRCLE-DIVIDING TEMPLATE

When creating any piece of jewelry that requires even, incremental markings, the circle-dividing template is an extremely handy tool. For example, you can use this template to lay out tabs for the Notched Interlock Bead (page 71) or to mark locations for decorating a double-dome bead.

MATERIALS

Brass or nickel sheet metal, 16 gauge,
   free of scratches

TOOLS & SUPPLIES

Jeweler's saw frame and 2/0 saw blades
Hand file, #2, 6 inches (15.2 cm)
Sandpaper, 400 grit
Scribe
Dividers
Steel ruler
Center punch
Plastic bag or envelop, 3 x 3 inches
   (7.6 x 7.6 cm) or larger

STEP BY STEP

1. Use the jeweler's saw to cut out a 3-inch (7.6 cm) square from the sheet metal. Make sure each corner of the square is at a 90-degree angle. File and sand each side of the metal square smooth and even.

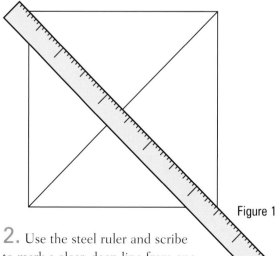

Figure 1

2. Use the steel ruler and scribe to mark a clear, deep line from one corner of the metal square to its diagonal corner. Repeat this process for the remaining two corners (figure 1). The intersection of these lines is the center of the square. Use the center punch to mark this point.

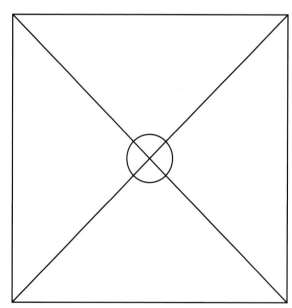

Figure 2

3. Set the tips of the dividers ¼ inch (6 mm) apart. Place one tip on the center punched mark made in step 2. Use the other tip to scribe a circle onto the sheet metal. There is now a circle with a ½-inch (1.3 cm) diameter in the center of the metal square (figure 2).

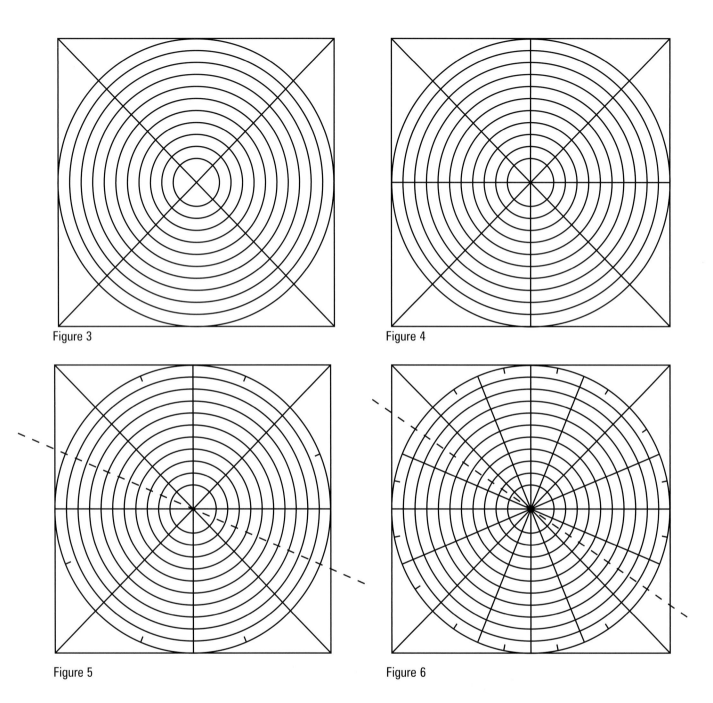

Figure 3

Figure 4

Figure 5

Figure 6

4. Increase the width between the tips of the dividers by ⅛ inch (3 mm). (The total space between tips is now ⅜ inch [1 cm].) Scribe this circle onto the metal square as directed in step 3.

5. Continue to increase the width between the tips of the dividers and scribe concentric circles onto the metal square until the last circle clears the perimeter of the square by ⅛ inch (3 mm) on each side as shown in figure 3.

6. Measure and mark the center point of each side of the metal square. The marks should be 1½ inches (3.8 cm) from the corners.

7. Using the ruler and the scribe, mark two clear, deep lines connecting the center marks of each side of the square. The template now has four straight lines, two diagonal ones from the corners and two from the center points of the sides (figure 4).

8. Measure and mark the midpoint between the straight scribed lines on the largest scribed circle on the metal square. There should be eight marked midpoints.

9. Using the ruler and scribe, connect all opposite marks made in step 8 with clear, deep lines (figure 5). Continue drawing these lines to the edges of the square.

10. Following the process described in step 8, measure and mark the midpoint on each segment of the largest circle. There are now 16 marked segments. As described in step 9, connect the opposite marks with a ruler and scribe, making clear, deep lines each time as shown in figure 6.

Tip

● Store your circle-dividing template in a plastic bag or envelop to keep it accurate, or drill a hole through one corner and hang it.

SAW BLADE SIZES

Blade Size	Blade Thickness	Blade Depth	Recommended Usage for Brown & Sharpe Gauge
8/0	0.0063 inch (0.16 mm)	0.0126 inch (0.32 mm)	up to 26
7/0	0.0067 inch (0.17 mm)	0.0130 inch (0.33 mm)	24–26
6/0	0.0070 inch (0.18 mm)	0.0140 inch (0.36 mm)	24
5/0	0.0080 inch (0.20 mm)	0.0157 inch (0.40 mm)	22–24
4/0	0.0086 inch (0.22 mm)	0.0175 inch (0.44 mm)	22
3/0	0.0095 inch (0.24 mm)	0.0190 inch (0.48 mm)	22
2/0	0.0103 inch (0.26 mm)	0.0204 inch (0.52 mm)	20–22
1/0	0.0110 inch (0.28 mm)	0.0220 inch (0.56 mm)	18–22
1	0.0120 inch (0.30 mm)	0.0240 inch (0.61 mm)	18–20
2	0.0134 inch (0.34 mm)	0.0276 inch (0.70 mm)	16–18
3	0.0140 inch (0.36 mm)	0.0290 inch (0.74 mm)	16–18
4	0.0150 inch (0.38 mm)	0.0307 inch (0.78 mm)	16–18
5	0.0158 inch (0.40 mm)	0.0331 inch (0.84 mm)	16
6	0.0173 inch (0.44 mm)	0.0370 inch (0.94 mm)	14
7	0.0189 inch (0.48 mm)	0.0400 inch (1.02 mm)	12
8	0.0197 inch (0.50 mm)	0.0440 inch (1.12 mm)	12

SOLDER FLOW & MELTING POINTS

Solder Type	Flow Point	Melting Point
Extra Easy	1145°F (618 °C)	1125°F (607 °C)
Easy	1325°F (718 °C)	1240°F (671 °C)
Medium	1360°F (737 °C)	1275°F (690 °C)
Hard	1450°F (787 °C)	1365°F (740 °C)

THE BROWN AND SHARPE (B. & S.) GAUGE FOR SHEET METAL		
Gauge Number	Thickness in inches	Thickness in millimeters
0	0.3249	8.2525
1	0.2893	7.3482
2	0.2576	6.5430
3	0.2294	5.8268
4	0.2043	5.1892
5	0.1819	4.6203
6	0.1620	4.1148
7	0.1443	3.6652
8	0.1285	3.2639
9	0.1144	2.9058
10	0.1019	2.5883
11	0.0907	2.3038
12	0.0808	2.0523
13	0.0720	1.8288
14	0.0641	1.6281
15	0.0571	1.4503
16	0.0508	1.2903
17	0.0453	1.1506
18	0.0403	1.0236
19	0.0359	0.9119
20	0.0320	0.8128
21	0.0285	0.7239
22	0.0253	0.6426
23	0.0226	0.5740
24	0.0201	0.5105
25	0.0179	0.4547
26	0.0159	0.4039
27	0.0142	0.3607
28	0.0126	0.3200
29	0.0113	0.2870
30	0.0100	0.2540

TWIST DRILL BIT DIAMETERS		
Bit Size	Inches	Millimeters
51	0.0670	1.70
52	0.0635	1.61
53	0.0595	1.51
54	0.0550	1.40
55	0.0520	1.32
56	0.0465	1.18
57	0.0430	1.09
58	0.0420	1.06
59	0.0410	1.04
60	0.0400	1.02
61	0.0390	0.99
62	0.0380	0.96
63	0.0370	0.94
64	0.0360	0.91
65	0.0350	0.89
66	0.0330	0.84
67	0.0320	0.81
68	0.0310	0.79
69	0.0292	0.74
70	0.0280	0.71
71	0.0260	0.66
72	0.0250	0.63
73	0.0240	0.61
74	0.0225	0.57
75	0.0210	0.53
76	0.0200	0.51
77	0.0180	0.46
78	0.0160	0.41
79	0.0145	0.37
80	0.0135	0.34

ACKNOWLEDGMENTS

Writing this book has been exciting, challenging, overwhelming at times, and a tremendous learning experience. It would be nearly impossible to thank all of the people, places, and things that have shaped me as an artist and brought me to the point where I was ready, willing, and able to take on this project. More specifically, I do have many people to thank for their help and support on different aspects of this endeavor from start to finish.

If it weren't for the love, support, and patience of my husband, Gary, this book would not have been possible. Through my anxieties, long irregular hours, and many interrupted schedules, he was there, steady, and ready to help.

Sue Burt helped me realize that I should and could take on writing a book about making metal beads. Thanks to her persistence, a fantasy became a reality.

I am very grateful to Kerstin Nichols for helping me network with other writers. At the onset of this project, I was feeling a bit lost and confused. Celie Fago, Linda Darty, and CeCe Wire graciously shared their expertise and wisdom about writing books. My communications with them were most valuable.

I cannot thank Cathy Heinz enough for all the help and support she gave me throughout this long process. Her skills as a writer combined with her metalsmithing knowledge, patience, and willingness to donate time were very useful, and I was so fortunate to have her guidance.

Thanks to Katie Cleaver, whose creativity has always been an inspiration to me. Our 20-year bead exchange is one of my most treasured series of events and collections.

Thanks to the staff at Lark Books. From my earliest communications with Nicole McConville, my long, well-organized, and informational conversations with Carol Taylor, to accommodations and legal questions answered patiently by Pat Wald, everyone was helpful and put me at ease. My editor, Marthe Le Van was always there to respond to me and guide me when needed. They all helped make writing the manuscript a smooth operation. Working with art director Kristi Pfeffer and photographers Steve Mann and Robert Diamante was a pleasure.

I am grateful to the many artists who contributed images of their beautiful work for this book. I feel fortunate to have such talented metalsmiths participate in this endeavor.

Cindy Eid was kind enough to offer her time and review the process pages. I respect her as a metalsmith and writer and thank her for helping me.

My life as an artist began long before I was a professional metalsmith. There are so many aspects of my everyday life that have subtly influenced me. It would be impossible to sort through and give specific thanks. I am so grateful to my family, friends, teachers, colleagues, and students who have always shown me love and support.

Because I had the good fortune of studying with many excellent teacher/mentors, I was inspired to teach others and share the traditional time-honored skills of metalsmithing. I owe a great deal to Philip Morton, Chuck Evans, Paul Mergen, and Bob Ebendorf. Teaching has been one of the most rewarding experiences I have ever had. I experience a constant exchange of knowledge and information when teaching. I am always stimulated and refreshed by others' creativity and ingenuity. All of this has enriched me and encouraged me to grow and take on new challenges. Thanks to so many.

INDEX

CONTRIBUTING ARTISTS

ABOUT THE AUTHOR

Pauline Warg is a metalsmith with more than 30 years of experience. Her artwork, be it jewelry or hollowware, incorporates precious and nonprecious metals, gems, and enamel. It is skillfully worked with great attention to detail using time-honored silversmithing techniques. Pauline holds a Bachelor of Fine Art from the University of Southern Maine, summa cum laude.

After completing her metalsmithing apprenticeship to master goldsmith Philip Morton, Pauline moved to Portsmouth, New Hampshire, and opened her business, Warg Designs. From 1983 to 1991, she designed lines of sterling silver tea accesories, specialty items for babies and children, and tableware for Shreve, Crump and Low of Boston, Massachusetts, and the affiliates of their parent company, Henry Birks and Sons.

From 1991 to 2001, Pauline developed, managed, and facilitated the Future Builders, Inc. metalsmithing program serving York and Cumberland Counties in Maine. Having attained her special education certification, she applied her metalsmithing expertise to a training program aimed at middle and high school students with behavioral impairments, emotional disorders, and learning disabilities.

Besides designing and creating wearable, functional, and sculptural objects, Pauline has taught metalsmithing at the Manchester Institute of Art, the University of New Hampshire, The Jewelry Institute, the Maine College of Art, and Metalwerx. Most recently, Pauline opened a new business, WARG Enamel & Tool Center, in Scarborough, Maine. The business has an expanded teaching studio for metalsmithing and enameling, as well as a tool and supply store.

Over the past 30 years, Pauline has won numerous awards and gained recognition for her metalsmithing and jewelry making, and her work has been exhibited nationally and internationally. Her first major award was Best in Show at the Toledo Museum of Art's May Show in 1975. In 2002, Pauline was given the Joe Tucker Metal Award at the League of New Hampshire Craftsmen's Annual "Living With Crafts" show and in 2005 she was awarded Best In Show, Jewelry at their exhibit "Craftwear." The Maine State Bar Association chose Pauline's brooch design as the Caroline Duby Glassman Award from 2004 to 2009.

Pauline is an artisan member of the Society of American Silversmiths, and a state juried member of the League of New Hampshire Craftsmen. She is also a member of the Enamelist's Society, and the Maine Crafts Association. Pauline has been included in *Who's Who of American Women*, *Who's Who in America*, and *Who's Who in the World* since 1997. She currently lives and works in southern Maine.